Python Geospatial Development Essentials

Utilize Python with open source libraries to build a lightweight, portable, and customizable GIS desktop application

Karim Bahgat

BIRMINGHAM - MUMBAI

Python Geospatial Development Essentials

First published: June 2015

Production reference: 1100615

Published by Packt Publishing Ltd.
Livery Place
35 Livery Street
Birmingham B3 2PB, UK.

ISBN 978-1-78217-540-7

www.packtpub.com

Credits

Author
Karim Bahgat

Reviewers
Gregory Giuliani
Jorge Samuel Mendes de Jesus
Athanasios Tom Kralidis
John Maurer
Adrian Vu

Commissioning Editor
Amarabha Banerjee

Acquisition Editors
Larissa Pinto
Rebecca Youé

Content Development Editor
Merwyn D'souza

Technical Editor
Prajakta Mhatre

Copy Editor
Charlotte Carneiro

Project Coordinator
Neha Bhatnagar

Proofreader
Safis Editing

Indexer
Rekha Nair

Production Coordinator
Manu Joseph

Cover Work
Manu Joseph

About the Author

Karim Bahgat holds an MA in peace and conflict transformation from the University of Tromsø in Norway, where he focused on the use of geographic information systems (GIS), opinion survey data, and open source programming tools in conflict studies. Since then, he has been employed as a research assistant for technical and geospatial work at the Peace Research Institute Oslo (PRIO) and the International Law and Policy Institute (ILPI). Karim was part of the early prototyping of the PRIO-GRID unified spatial data structure for social science and conflict research, and is currently helping develop a new updated version (`https://www.prio.org/Data/PRIO-GRID/`).

His main use of technology, as a developer, has been with Python programming, geospatial tools and mapping, the geocoding of textual data, data visualization, application development, and some web technology. Karim is the author of a journal article publication, numerous data- and GIS-oriented Python programming libraries, the Easy Georeferencer free geocoding software, and several related technical websites, including `www.pythongisresources.wordpress.com`.

I am very grateful for the detailed feedback, suggestions, and troubleshooting of chapters from the reviewers; the encouragement and guidance from the publisher's administrators and staff, and the patience and encouragement from friends, family, colleagues, and loved ones (especially my inspirational sidekicks, Laura and Murdock). I also want to thank all my teachers at the Chapman University and University of North Dakota, who got me here in the first place. They helped me think out of the box and led me into this wonderful world of geospatial technology.

About the Reviewers

Gregory Giuliani is a geologist with a PhD in environmental sciences (theme: spatial data infrastructure for the environment). He is a senior scientific associate at the University of Geneva (Switzerland) and the focal point for spatial data infrastructure (SDI) at GRID-Geneva. He is the manager of the EU/FP7 EOPOWER project and the work package leader in the EU/FP7 enviroGRIDS and AfroMaison projects, where he coordinates SDI development and implementation. He also participated in the EU/FP7 ACQWA project and is the GRID-Geneva lead developer of the PREVIEW Global Risk Data Platform (`http://preview.grid.unep.ch`). He coordinates and develops capacity building material on SDI for enviroGRIDS and actively participates and contributes to various activities of the Global Earth Observation System of Systems (GEOSS). Specialized in OGC standards, interoperability, and brokering technology for environmental data and services, he is the coordinator of the Task ID-02 "Developing Institutional and Individual Capacity" for GEO/GEOSS.

Jorge Samuel Mendes de Jesus has 15 years of programming experience in the field of Geoinformatics, with a focus on Python programming, OGC web services, and spatial databases.

He has a PhD in geography and sustainable development from Ben-Gurion University of the Negev, Israel. He has been employed by the Joint Research Center (JRC), Italy, where he worked on projects such as EuroGEOSS, Intamap, and Digital Observatory for Protected Areas (DOPA). He continued his professional career at Plymouth Marine Laboratory, UK, as a member of the Remote Sensing Group contributing to the NETMAR project and actively promoting the implementation of the WSDL standard in PyWPS. He currently works at ISRIC—World Soil Information in the Netherlands, where he supports the development of Global Soil Information Facilities (GSIF).

Athanasios Tom Kralidis is a senior systems scientist for the Meteorological Service of Canada, where he provides geospatial technical and architectural leadership in support of MSC's data. Tom's professional background includes key involvement in the development and integration of geospatial standards, systems, and services for the Canadian Geospatial Data Infrastructure (CGDI) with Natural Resources Canada. He also uses these principles in architecting RésEau, Canada's water information portal. Tom is the lead architect of the renewal of the World Ozone and Ultraviolet Radiation Data Centre (WOUDC) in support of the WMO Global Atmospheric Watch.

Tom is active in the Open Geospatial Consortium (OGC) community, and was lead contributor to the OGC Web Map Context Documents Specification. He was also a member of the CGDI Architecture Advisory Board, as well as part of the Canadian Advisory Committee to ISO Technical Committee 211 Geographic information/Geomatics.

Tom is a developer on the MapServer, GeoNode, QGIS, and OWSLib open source software projects, and part of the MapServer Project Steering Committee. He is the founder and lead developer of `pycsw`, an OGC-compliant CSW reference implementation. Tom is a charter member of the Open Source Geospatial Foundation. He holds a bachelor's degree in geography from York University, a GIS certification from Algonquin College, and a master's degree in geography and environmental studies (research and dissertation in geospatial web services/infrastructure) from Carleton University. Tom is a certified Geomatics Specialist (GIS/LIS) with the Canadian Institute of Geomatics.

John Maurer is a programmer and data manager at the Pacific Islands Ocean Observing System (PacIOOS) in Honolulu, Hawaii. He creates and configures web interfaces and data services to provide access, visualization, and mapping of oceanographic data from a variety of sources, including satellite remote sensing, forecast models, GIS layers, and in situ observations (buoys, sensors, shark tracking, and so on) throughout the insular Pacific. He obtained a graduate certificate in remote sensing, as well as a master's degree in geography from the University of Colorado at Boulder, where he developed software to analyze ground-penetrating radar (GPR) for snow accumulation measurements on the Greenland ice sheet. While in Boulder, he worked with the National Snow and Ice Data Center (NSIDC) for 8 years, sparking his initial interest in earth science and all things geospatial; an unexpected but comfortable detour from his undergraduate degree in music, science, and technology at Stanford University.

Adrian Vu is a web and mobile developer based in Singapore, and has over 10 years of experience working on various projects for start-ups and organizations. He holds a BSc in information systems management (majoring in business intelligence and analytics) from Singapore Management University. Occasionally, he likes to dabble in new frameworks and technologies, developing many useful apps for all to use and play with.

www.PacktPub.com

Support files, eBooks, discount offers, and more

For support files and downloads related to your book, please visit www.PacktPub.com.

Did you know that Packt offers eBook versions of every book published, with PDF and ePub files available? You can upgrade to the eBook version at www.PacktPub.com and as a print book customer, you are entitled to a discount on the eBook copy. Get in touch with us at service@packtpub.com for more details.

At www.PacktPub.com, you can also read a collection of free technical articles, sign up for a range of free newsletters and receive exclusive discounts and offers on Packt books and eBooks.

https://www2.packtpub.com/books/subscription/packtlib

Do you need instant solutions to your IT questions? PacktLib is Packt's online digital book library. Here, you can search, access, and read Packt's entire library of books.

Why subscribe?

- Fully searchable across every book published by Packt
- Copy and paste, print, and bookmark content
- On demand and accessible via a web browser

Free access for Packt account holders

If you have an account with Packt at www.PacktPub.com, you can use this to access PacktLib today and view 9 entirely free books. Simply use your login credentials for immediate access.

Table of Contents

Preface

Python has become the language of choice for many in the geospatial industry. Some use Python as a way to automate their workflows in software, such as ArcGIS or QGIS. Others play around with the nuts and bolts of Python's immense variety of third-party open source geospatial toolkits.

Given all the programming tools available and the people already familiar with geospatial software, there is no reason why you should have to choose either one or the other. Programmers can now develop their own applications from scratch to better suit their needs. Python is, after all, known as a language for rapid development.

By developing your own application, you can have fun with it, experiment with new visual layouts and creative designs, create platforms for specialized workflows, and tailor to the needs of others.

What this book covers

Chapter 1, Preparing to Build Your Own GIS Application, talks about the benefits of developing a custom geospatial application and describes how to set up your development environment, and create your application folder structure.

Chapter 2, Accessing Geodata, implements the crucial data loading and saving capabilities of your application for both vector and raster data.

Chapter 3, Designing the Visual Look of Our Application, creates and puts together the basic building blocks of your application's user interface, giving you a first look at what your application will look like.

Chapter 4, Rendering Our Geodata, adds rendering capabilities so that the user can interactively view, zoom, and pan data inside the application.

Chapter 5, *Managing and Organizing Geographic Data*, creates a basic functionality for splitting, merging, and cleaning both the vector and raster data.

Chapter 6, *Analyzing Geographic Data*, develops basic analysis functionality, such as overlay statistics, for vector and raster data.

Chapter 7, *Packaging and Distributing Your Application*, wraps it all up by showing you how to share and distribute your application, so it is easier for you or others to use it.

Chapter 8, *Looking Forward*, considers how you may wish to proceed to further build on, customize, and extend your basic application into something more elaborate or specialized in whichever way you want.

What you need for this book

There are no real requirements for this book. However, to keep the book short and sweet, the instructions assume that you have a Windows operating system. If you are on Mac OS X or Linux, you should still be able create and run the application, but then you will have to figure out the equivalent installation instructions for your operating system. You may be forced to deal with compiling C++ code and face the potential of unexpected errors. All other installations will be covered throughout the book, including which Python version to use.

Who this book is for

This book is ideal for Python programmers and software developers who are tasked with or wish to make a customizable special-purpose GIS application, or are interested in expanding their knowledge of working with spatial data cleaning, analysis, or map visualization. Analysts, political scientists, geographers, and GIS specialists seeking a creative platform to experiment with cutting-edge spatial analysis, but are still only beginners in Python, will also find this book beneficial. Familiarity with Tkinter application development in Python is preferable but not mandatory.

Conventions

In this book, you will find a number of text styles that distinguish between different kinds of information. Here are some examples of these styles and an explanation of their meaning.

Code words in text, database table names, folder names, filenames, file extensions, pathnames, dummy URLs, user input, and Twitter handles are shown as follows: "Download the Shapely wheel file that fits our system, looking something like `Shapely-1.5.7-cp27-none-win32.whl`."

A block of code is set as follows:

```
class LayerGroup:
    def __init__(self):
        self.layers = list()
        self.connected_maps = list()

    def __iter__(self):
        for layer in self.layers:
            yield layer

    def add_layer(self, layer):
        self.layers.append(layer)

    def move_layer(self, from_pos, to_pos):
        layer = self.layers.pop(from_pos)
        self.layers.insert(to_pos, layer)

    def remove_layer(self, position):
        self.layers.pop(position)

    def get_position(self, layer):
        return self.layers.index(layer)
```

Any command-line input or output is written as follows:

```
>>> import PIL, PIL.Image
>>> img = PIL.Image.open("your/path/to/icon.png")
>>> img.save("your/path/to/pythongis/app/icon.ico",
sizes=[(255,255),(128,128),(64,64),(48,48),(32,32),(16,16),(8,8)])
```

New terms and **important words** are shown in bold. Words that you see on the screen, for example, in menus or dialog boxes, appear in the text like this: "Click on the **Inno Setup** link on the left side."

 Warnings or important notes appear in a box like this.

Tips and tricks appear like this.

Reader feedback

Feedback from our readers is always welcome. Let us know what you think about this book—what you liked or disliked. Reader feedback is important for us as it helps us develop titles that you will really get the most out of.

To send us general feedback, simply e-mail feedback@packtpub.com, and mention the book's title in the subject of your message.

If there is a topic that you have expertise in and you are interested in either writing or contributing to a book, see our author guide at www.packtpub.com/authors.

Customer support

Now that you are the proud owner of a Packt book, we have a number of things to help you to get the most from your purchase.

Downloading the example code

You can download the example code files from your account at http://www.packtpub.com for all the Packt Publishing books you have purchased. If you purchased this book elsewhere, you can visit http://www.packtpub.com/support and register to have the files e-mailed directly to you.

Errata

Although we have taken every care to ensure the accuracy of our content, mistakes do happen. If you find a mistake in one of our books—maybe a mistake in the text or the code—we would be grateful if you could report this to us. By doing so, you can save other readers from frustration and help us improve subsequent versions of this book. If you find any errata, please report them by visiting http://www.packtpub.com/submit-errata, selecting your book, clicking on the **Errata Submission Form** link, and entering the details of your errata. Once your errata are verified, your submission will be accepted and the errata will be uploaded to our website or added to any list of existing errata under the Errata section of that title.

To view the previously submitted errata, go to `https://www.packtpub.com/books/content/support` and enter the name of the book in the search field. The required information will appear under the **Errata** section.

Piracy

Piracy of copyrighted material on the Internet is an ongoing problem across all media. At Packt, we take the protection of our copyright and licenses very seriously. If you come across any illegal copies of our works in any form on the Internet, please provide us with the location address or website name immediately so that we can pursue a remedy.

Please contact us at `copyright@packtpub.com` with a link to the suspected pirated material.

We appreciate your help in protecting our authors and our ability to bring you valuable content.

Questions

If you have a problem with any aspect of this book, you can contact us at `questions@packtpub.com`, and we will do our best to address the problem.

1
Preparing to Build Your Own GIS Application

You are here because you love Python programming and are interested in making your own **Geographic Information Systems** (**GIS**) application. You want to create a desktop application, in other words, a user interface, that helps you or others create, process, analyze, and visualize geographic data. This book will be your step-by-step guide toward that goal.

We assume that you are someone who enjoys programming and being creative but are not necessarily a computer science guru, Python expert, or seasoned GIS analyst. To successfully proceed with this book, it is recommended that you have a basic introductory knowledge of Python programming that includes classes, methods, and the **Tkinter** toolkit, as well as some core GIS concepts. If you are a newcomer to some of these, we will still cover some of the basics, but you will need to have the interest and ability to follow along at a fast pace.

In this introductory chapter, you will cover the following:

- Learn some of the benefits of creating a GIS application from scratch
- Set up your computer, so you can follow the book instructions.
- Become familiar with the roadmap toward creating our application.

Why reinvent the wheel?

The first step in preparing ourselves for this book is in convincing ourselves why we want to make our own GIS application, as well as to be clear about our motives. Spatial analysis and GIS have been popular for decades and there is plenty of GIS software out there, so why go through the trouble of reinventing the wheel? Firstly, we aren't really reinventing the wheel, since Python can be extended with plenty of third-party libraries that take care of most of our geospatial needs (more on that later).

For me, the main motivation stems from the problem that most of today's GIS applications are aimed at highly capable and technical users who are well-versed in GIS or computer science, packed with a dizzying array of buttons and options that will scare off many an analyst. We believe that there is a virtue in trying to create a simpler and more user-friendly software for beginner GIS users or even the broader public, without having to start completely from scratch. This way, we also add more alternatives for users to choose from, as supplements to the current GIS market dominated by a few major giants, notably ArcGIS and QGIS, but also others such as GRASS, uDig, gvSIG, and more.

Another particularly exciting reason to create your own GIS from scratch is to make your own domain-specific special purpose software for any task you can imagine, whether it is a water flow model GIS, an ecological migrations GIS, or even a GIS for kids. Such specialized tasks that would usually require many arduous steps in an ordinary GIS, could be greatly simplified into a single button and accompanied with suitable functionality, design layout, icons, and colors. One such example is the **Crime Analytics for Space-Time (CAST)** software produced by the GeoDa Center at Arizona State University, seen in the following picture:

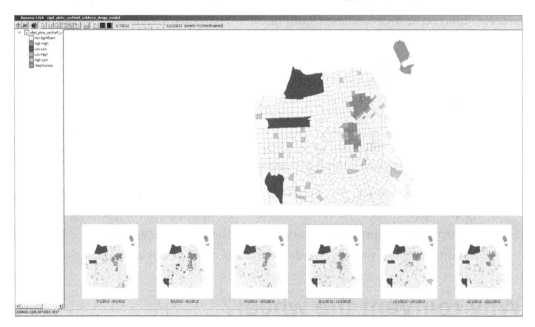

Also, by creating your GIS from scratch, it is possible to have greater control of the size and portability of your application. This can enable you to go small—letting your application have faster startup time, and travel the Internet or on a USB-stick easily. Although storage space itself is not as much of an issue these days, from a user's perspective, installing a 200 MB application is still a greater psychological investment with a greater toll in terms of willingness to try it than a mere 30 MB application (all else being equal). This is particularly true in the realm of smartphones and tablets, a very exciting market for special-purpose geospatial apps. While the specific application we make in this book will not be able to run on iOS or Android devices, it will run on Windows 8-based hybrid tablets, and can be rebuilt around a different GUI toolkit in order to support iOS or Android (we will mention some very brief suggestions for this in *Chapter 8, Looking Forward*).

Finally, the utility and philosophy of free and open source software may be an important motivation for some of you. Many people today, learn to appreciate open source GIS after losing access to subscription-based applications like ArcGIS when they complete their university education or change their workplace. By developing your own open source GIS application and sharing with others, you can contribute back to and become part of the community that once helped you.

Setting up your computer

In this book, we follow steps on how to make an application that is developed in a Windows environment. This does not mean that the application cannot be developed on Mac OS X or Linux, but those platforms may have slightly different installation instructions and may require compiling of the binary code that is outside the scope of this book. Therefore, we leave that choice up to the reader. In this book, which focuses on Windows, we avoid the problem of compiling it altogether, using precompiled versions where possible (more on this later).

The development process itself will be done using Python 2.7, specifically the 32-bit version, though 64-bit can theoretically be used as well (note that this is the bit version of your Python installation and has nothing to do with the bit version of your operating system). Although there exists many newer versions, version 2.7 is the most widely supported in terms of being able to use third-party packages. It has also been reported that the version 2.7 will continue to be actively developed and promoted until the year 2020. It will still be possible to use after support has ended. If you do not already have version 2.7, install it now, by following these steps:

1. Go to `https://www.python.org/`.

2. Under **Downloads** click on download the latest 32-bit version of Python 2.7 for Windows, which at the time of this writing is Python 2.7.9.

3. Download and run the installation program.

For the actual code writing and editing, we will be using the built-in **Python Interactive Development Environment** (IDLE), but you may of course use any code editor you want. The IDLE lets you write long scripts that can be saved to files and offers an interactive shell window to execute one line at a time. There should be a desktop or start-menu link to Python IDLE after installing Python.

Installing third-party packages

In order to make our application, we will have to rely on the rich and varied ecosystem of third-party packages that already exists for GIS usage.

> **The Python Package Index** (PyPI) website currently lists more than 240 packages tagged **Topic :: Scientific/Engineering :: GIS**. For a less overwhelming overview of the more popular GIS-related Python libraries, check out the catalogue at the *Python-GIS-Resources* website created by the author:
>
> http://pythongisresources.wordpress.com/

We will have to define which packages to use and install, and this depends on the type of application we are making. What we want to make in this book is a lightweight, highly portable, extendable, and general-purpose GIS application. For these reasons, we avoid heavy packages like GDAL, NumPy, Matplotlib, SciPy, and Mapnik (weighing in at about 30 MB each or about 150-200 MB if we combine them all together). Instead, we focus on lighter third-party packages specialized for each specific functionality.

> Dropping these heavy packages is a bold decision, as they contain a lot of functionality, and are reliable, efficient, and a dependency for many other packages. If you decide that you want to use them in an application where size is not an issue, you may want to begin now by installing the multipurpose NumPy and possibly SciPy, both of which have easy-to-use installers from their official websites. The other heavy packages will be briefly revisited in later chapters.

Specific installation instructions are given for each package in the chapter where they are relevant (see the following table for an overview) so that if you do not want certain functionalities, you can ignore those installations. Due to our focus to make a basic and lightweight application, we will only be installing a small number of packages. However, we will provide suggestions throughout the book about other relevant packages that you may wish to add later on.

Chapter	Installation	Purpose
1	Python	
1	PIL	Raster data, management, and analysis
1	Shapely	Vector management and analysis
2	PyShp	Data
2	PyGeoj	Data
2	Rtree	Vector data speedup
4	PyAgg	Visualization
7	Py2exe	Application distribution

The typical way to install Python packages is using `pip` (included with Python 2.7), which downloads and installs packages directly from the Python Package Index website. `Pip` is used in the following way:

- Step 1 — open your operating system's command line (not the Python IDLE). On Windows, this is done by searching your system for `cmd.exe` and running it.

- Step 2 — in the black screen window that pops up, one simply types `pip install packagename`. This will only work if `pip` is on your system's environment path. If this is not the case, a quick fix is to simply type the full path to the `pip` script `C:\Python27\Scripts\pip` instead of just `pip`.

For C or C++ based packages, it is becoming increasingly popular to make them available as precompiled **wheel** files ending in `.whl`, which has caused some confusion on how to install them. Luckily, we can use `pip` to install these wheel files as well, by simply downloading the wheel and pointing `pip` to its file path.

Since some of our dependencies have multiple purposes and are not unique to just one chapter, we will install these ones now. One of them is the **Python Imaging Library (PIL)**, which we will use for the raster data model and for visualization. Let's go ahead and install PIL for Windows now:

1. Go to `https://pypi.python.org/pypi/Pillow/2.6.1`.

2. Click on the latest `.exe` file link for our 32-bit Python 2.7 environment to download the PIL installer, which is currently `Pillow-2.6.1.win32-py2.7.exe`.

3. Run the installation file.

4. Open the IDLE interactive shell and type `import PIL` to make sure it was installed correctly.

Another central package we will be using is Shapely, used for location testing and geometric manipulation. To install it on Windows, perform the following steps:

1. Go to `http://www.lfd.uci.edu/~gohlke/pythonlibs/#shapely`.

2. Download the Shapely wheel file that fits our system, looking something like `Shapely-1.5.7-cp27-none-win32.whl`.

3. As described earlier, open a command line window and type `C:\Python27\Scripts\pip install path\to\Shapely-1.5.7-cp27-none-win32.whl` to unpack the precompiled binaries.

4. To make sure it was installed correctly, open the IDLE interactive shell and type `import shapely`.

Imagining the roadmap ahead

Before we begin developing our application, it is important that we create a vision of how we want to structure our application. In Python terms, we will be creating a multilevel package with various subpackages and submodules to take care of different parts of our functionality, independently of any user interface. Only on top of this underlying functionality do we create the visual user interface as a way to access and run that underlying code. This way, we build a solid system, and allow power-users to access all the same functionality via Python scripting for greater automation and efficiency, as exists for ArcGIS and QGIS.

To setup the main Python package behind our application, create a new folder called `pythongis` anywhere on your computer. For Python to be able to interpret the folder `pythongis` as an importable package, it needs to find a file named __init__.py in that folder. Perform the following steps:

1. Open **Python IDLE** from the Windows start menu.

2. The first window to pop up is the interactive shell. To open the script editing window click on **File** and **New**.

3. Click on **File** and then **Save As**.

4. In the dialog window that pops up, browse into the `pythongis` folder, type __init__.py as the filename, and click on **Save**.

There are two main types of GIS data: **vector** (coordinate-based geometries such as points, lines, and polygons) and **raster** (a regularly spaced out grid of data points or cells, similar to an image and its pixels).

For a more detailed introduction to the differences between vector and raster data, and other basic GIS concepts, we refer the reader to the book *Learning Geospatial Analysis with Python*, by Joel Lawhead. You can find this book at:

```
https://www.packtpub.com/application-development/
learning-geospatial-analysis-python
```

Since vector and raster data are so fundamentally different in all regards, we split our package in two, one for vector and one for raster. Using the same method as earlier, we create two new subpackage folders within the `pythongis` package; one called `vector` and one called `raster` (each with the same aforementioned empty `__init__.py` file). Thus, the structure of our package will look as follows (note that `: package` is not part of the folder name):

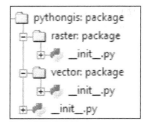

To make our new `vector` and `raster` subpackages importable by our top level `pythongis` package, we need to add the following relative import statements in `pythongis/__init__.py`:

```
from . import vector
from . import raster
```

Throughout the course of this book, we will build the functionality of these two data types as a set of Python modules in their respective folders. Eventually, we want to end up with a GIS application that has only the most basic of geospatial tools so that we will be able to load, save, manage, visualize, and overlay data, each of which will be covered in the following chapters.

As far as our final product goes, since we focus on clarity and simplicity, we do not put too much effort into making it fast or memory efficient. This comes from an often repeated saying among programmers, an example of which is found in *Structured Programming with go to Statements*, ACM, Computing Surveys 6 (4):

premature optimization is the root of all evil

– Donald E. Knuth

This leaves us with software that works best with small files, which in most cases is good enough. Once you have a working application and you feel that you need support for larger or faster files, then it's up to you if you want to put in the extra effort of optimization.

The GIS application you end up with at the end of the book is simple but functional, and is meant to serve as a framework that you can easily build on. To leave you with some ideas to pick up on, we placed various information boxes throughout the book with ways that you can optimize or extend your application. For any of the core topics and features that we were not able to cover earlier in the book, we give a broader discussion of missing functionality and future suggestions in the final chapter.

Summary

In this chapter, you learned about why you want to create a GIS application using Python, set up our programming environment, installed some recurring packages, and created your application structure and framework.

In the next chapter, you will take the first step toward making a geospatial application, by creating a simple yet powerful module for loading and saving some common geospatial data formats from scratch.

2
Accessing Geodata

All GIS processing must start with geographic data, so we begin our application by building the capacity to interact with, load, and save various geographic file formats. This chapter is divided into a vector and raster section, and in each section, we will cover the following:

- Firstly, we create a data interface which means understanding data structures and how to interact with them.

- Secondly and thirdly, any format-specific differences are outsourced to separate loader and saver modules.

This is a lot of functionality to fit into one chapter, but by working your way through, you will learn a lot about data structures, and file formats, and end up with a solid foundation for your application.

The approach

In our efforts to build data access in this chapter, we focus on simplicity, understanding, and lightweight libraries. We create standardized data interfaces for vector and raster data so that we can use the same methods and expect the same results on any data, without worrying about file format differences. They are not necessarily optimized for speed or memory efficiency as they load entire files into memory at once.

In our choice of third-party libraries for loading and saving, we focus on format-specific ones, so that we can pick and choose which formats to support and thus maintain a lightweight application. This requires some more work but allows us to learn intricate details about file formats.

If the size is not an issue in your application, you may wish to instead use the more powerful **GDAL** library, which can single-handedly load and save a much wider range of both vector and raster formats. To use GDAL, I suggest downloading and installing a precompiled version from http://www.lfd.uci.edu/~gohlke/pythonlibs/#gdal. On top of GDAL, the packages **Fiona** (http://www.lfd.uci.edu/~gohlke/pythonlibs/#fiona) and **Rasterio** (http://www.lfd.uci.edu/~gohlke/pythonlibs/#rasterio) provide a more convenient and Pythonic interface to GDAL's functionality for vector and raster data, respectively.

Vector data

We begin by adding support for vector data. We will be creating three submodules inside our vector package: data, loader, and saver. To make these accessible from their parent vector package, we need to import it in vector/__init__.py as follows:

```
from . import data
from . import loader
from . import saver
```

A data interface for vector data

The first thing we want is a data interface that we can conveniently interact with. This data interface will be contained in a module of its own, so create this module now and save it as vector/data.py.

We start off with a few basic imports, including compatibility functions for Shapely (which we installed in *Chapter 1, Preparing to Build Your Own GIS Application*) and the spatial indexing abilities of **Rtree**, a package we will install later. Note that vector data loading and saving, are handled by separate modules that we have not yet created, but since they are accessed through our data interface, we need to import them here:

```
# import builtins
import sys, os, itertools, operator
from collections import OrderedDict
import datetime

# import shapely geometry compatibility functions
# ...and rename them for clarity
import shapely
from shapely.geometry import asShape as geojson2shapely
```

```
# import rtree for spatial indexing
import rtree

# import internal modules
from . import loader
from . import saver
```

Downloading the example code

You can download the example code files from your account at http://www.packtpub.com for all the Packt Publishing books you have purchased. If you purchased this book elsewhere, you can visit http://www.packtpub.com/support and register to have the files e-mailed directly to you.

The vector data structure

Geographic vector data can be thought of as a table of data. Each row in the table is an observation (say, a country), and holds one or more attributes, or piece of information for that observation (say, population). In a vector data structure, rows are known as a **features**, and have additional geometry definitions (coordinates that define, say, the shape and location of a country). An overview of the structure may therefore look something like this:

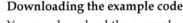

	VectorData				
	Field	Field	Field	Field	
Feature	Value	Value	Value	Value	Geometry
Feature	Value	Value	Value	Value	Geometry
Feature	Value	Value	Value	Value	Geometry
Feature	Value	Value	Value	Value	Geometry

In our implementation of the vector data structure, we therefore create the interface as a VectorData class. To create and populate a VectorData instance with data, we can give it a filepath argument that it loads via the loader module that we create later. We also allow for optional keyword arguments to pass to the loader, which as we shall see includes the ability to specify text encoding. Alternatively, an empty VectorData instance can be created by not passing it any arguments. While creating an empty instance, it is possible to specify the geometry type of the entire data instance (meaning, it can only hold either polygon, line, or point geometries), otherwise it will set the data type based on the geometry type of the first feature that is added.

In addition to storing the fieldnames and creating features from rows and geometries, a VectorData instance remembers the filepath origin of the loaded data if applicable, and the **Coordinate Reference System (CRS)** which defaults to unprojected WGS84 if not specified.

To store the features, rather than using lists or dictionaries, we use an **ordered** dictionary that allows us to identify each feature with a unique ID, sort the features, and perform fast and frequent feature lookups. To ensure that each feature in VectorData has a unique ID, we define a unique ID generator and attach independent ID generator instances to each VectorData instance.

To let us interact with the VectorData instance, we add various magic methods to enable standard Python operations such as getting the number of features in the data, looping through them, and getting and setting them through indexing their ID. Finally, we include a convenient add_feature and copy method. Take a look at the following code:

```python
def ID_generator():
    i = 0
    while True:
        yield i
        i += 1


class VectorData:
    def __init__(self, filepath=None, type=None, **kwargs):
        self.filepath = filepath

        # type is optional and will make the features ensure that
all geometries are of that type
        # if None, type enforcement will be based on first
geometry found
        self.type = type

        if filepath:
            fields,rows,geometries,crs =
loader.from_file(filepath, **kwargs)
        else:
            fields,rows,geometries,crs = [],[],[],"+proj=longlat
+ellps=WGS84 +datum=WGS84 +no_defs"

        self.fields = fields

        self._id_generator = ID_generator()
```

```
        ids_rows_geoms =
itertools.izip(self._id_generator,rows,geometries)
        featureobjs = (Feature(self,row,geom,id=id) for
id,row,geom in ids_rows_geoms )
        self.features = OrderedDict([ (feat.id,feat) for feat in
featureobjs ])
        self.crs = crs

    def __len__(self):
        """
        How many features in data.
        """
        return len(self.features)

    def __iter__(self):
        """
        Loop through features in order.
        """
        for feat in self.features.itervalues():
            yield feat

    def __getitem__(self, i):
        """
        Get a Feature based on its feature id.
        """
        if isinstance(i, slice):
            raise Exception("Can only get one feature at a time")
        else:
            return self.features[i]

    def __setitem__(self, i, feature):
        """
        Set a Feature based on its feature id.
        """
        if isinstance(i, slice):
            raise Exception("Can only set one feature at a time")
        else:
            self.features[i] = feature

    ### DATA ###

    def add_feature(self, row, geometry):
        feature = Feature(self, row, geometry)
        self[feature.id] = feature
```

```
    def copy(self):
        new = VectorData()
        new.fields = [field for field in self.fields]
        featureobjs = (Feature(new, feat.row, feat.geometry) for
feat in self )
        new.features = OrderedDict([ (feat.id,feat) for feat in
featureobjs ])
        if hasattr(self, "spindex"): new.spindex =
self.spindex.copy()
        return new
```

When we load or add features, they are stored in a `Feature` class with a link to its parent `VectorData` class. For the sake of simplicity, maximum interoperability, and memory efficiency, we choose to store feature geometries in the popular and widely supported **GeoJSON** format, which is just a Python dictionary structure formatted according to certain rules.

> GeoJSON is a human-readable textual representation to describe various vector geometries, such as points, lines, and polygons. For the full specification, go to `http://geojson.org/geojson-spec.html`.

We make sure to give the `Feature` class some magic methods to support standard Python operations, such as easy getting and setting of attributes through fieldname indexing using the position of the desired field in the feature's parent list of fields to fetch the relevant row value. A `get_shapely` method to return the Shapely geometry representation and `copy` method will also be useful for later. The following code explains the `Feature` class:

```
class Feature:
    def __init__(self, data, row, geometry, id=None):
        "geometry must be a geojson dictionary"
        self._data = data
        self.row  = list(row)

        self.geometry = geometry.copy()

        # ensure it is same geometry type as parent
        geotype = self.geometry["type"]
        if self._data.type:
            if "Point" in geotype and self._data.type == "Point":
pass
            elif "LineString" in geotype and self._data.type ==
"LineString": pass
```

```
          elif "Polygon" in geotype and self._data.type ==
"Polygon": pass
          else: raise TypeError("Each feature geometry must be
of the same type as the file it is attached to")
      else: self._data.type =
self.geometry["type"].replace("Multi", "")

      if id == None: id = next(self._data._id_generator)
      self.id = id

  def __getitem__(self, i):
      if isinstance(i, (str,unicode)):
          i = self._data.fields.index(i)
      return self.row[i]

  def __setitem__(self, i, setvalue):
      if isinstance(i, (str,unicode)):
          i = self._data.fields.index(i)
      self.row[i] = setvalue

  def get_shapely(self):
      return geojson2shapely(self.geometry)

  def copy(self):
      geoj = self.geometry
      if self._cached_bbox: geoj["bbox"] = self._cached_bbox
      return Feature(self._data, self.row, geoj)
```

Computing bounding boxes

Although we now have the basic structure of vector data, we want some additional
convenience methods. For vector data, it is frequently useful to know the **bounding
box** of each feature, which is an aggregated geographical description of a feature
represented as a sequence of four coordinates [xmin, ymin, xmax, ymax].
Computing the bounding box can be computationally expensive, so we allow the
Feature instance to receive a precomputed bounding box upon instantiation if
available. In the Feature's __init__ method, we therefore add to what we have
already written:

```
      bbox = geometry.get("bbox")
      self._cached_bbox = bbox
```

This bounding box can also be cached or stored, for later use, so that we can just keep referring to that value after we have computed it. Using the @property descriptor, before we define the Feature class's bbox method, allows us to access the bounding box as a simple value or attribute even though it is computed as several steps in a method:

```
@property
def bbox(self):
    if not self._cached_bbox:
        geotype = self.geometry["type"]
        coords = self.geometry["coordinates"]

        if geotype == "Point":
            x,y = coords
            bbox = [x,y,x,y]
        elif geotype in ("MultiPoint","LineString"):
            xs, ys = itertools.izip(*coords)
            bbox = [min(xs),min(ys),max(xs),max(ys)]
        elif geotype == "MultiLineString":
            xs = [x for line in coords for x,y in line]
            ys = [y for line in coords for x,y in line]
            bbox = [min(xs),min(ys),max(xs),max(ys)]
        elif geotype == "Polygon":
            exterior = coords[0]
            xs, ys = itertools.izip(*exterior)
            bbox = [min(xs),min(ys),max(xs),max(ys)]
        elif geotype == "MultiPolygon":
            xs = [x for poly in coords for x,y in poly[0]]
            ys = [y for poly in coords for x,y in poly[0]]
            bbox = [min(xs),min(ys),max(xs),max(ys)]
        self._cached_bbox = bbox
    return self._cached_bbox
```

Finally, the bounding box for the entire collection of features in the VectorData class is also useful, so we create a similar routine at the VectorData level, except we do not care about caching because a VectorData class will frequently lose or gain new features. We want the bounding box to always be up to date. Add the following dynamic property to the VectorData class:

```
@property
def bbox(self):
    xmins, ymins, xmaxs, ymaxs = itertools.izip(*(feat.bbox
for feat in self))
    xmin, xmax = min(xmins), max(xmaxs)
    ymin, ymax = min(ymins), max(ymaxs)
    bbox = (xmin, ymin, xmax, ymax)
    return bbox
```

Spatial indexing

Finally, we add a spatial indexing structure that nests the bounding boxes of overlapping features inside each other so that feature locations can be tested and retrieved faster. For this, we will use the Rtree library. Perform the following steps:

1. Go to `http://www.lfd.uci.edu/~gohlke/pythonlibs/#rtree`.

2. Download the wheel file appropriate for our system, currently `Rtree-0.8.2.-cp27-none-win32.whl`.

3. To install the package on Windows, open your command line and type `C:/Python27/Scripts/pip install path/to/Rtree-0.8.2.-cp27-none-win32.whl`.

4. To verify that the installation has worked, open an interactive Python shell window and type `import rtree`.

 Rtree is only one type of spatial index. Another common one is a **Quad Tree** index, whose main advantage is faster updating of the index if you need to change it often. `PyQuadTree` is a pure-Python implementation created by the author, which you can install in the command line as `C:/Python27/Scripts/pip install pyquadtree`.

Since spatial indexes rely on bounding boxes, which as we said before can be computationally costly, we only create the spatial index if the user specifically asks for it. Therefore, let's create a `VectorData` class method that will make a spatial index from the Rtree library, populate it by inserting the bounding boxes of each feature and their ID, and store it as a property. This is shown in the following code snippet:

```
def create_spatial_index(self):
    """Allows quick overlap search methods"""
    self.spindex = rtree.index.Index()
    for feat in self:
        self.spindex.insert(feat.id, feat.bbox)
```

Once created, Rtree's spatial index has two main methods that can be used for fast spatial lookups. The spatial lookups only return the IDs of the matches, so we use those IDs to fetch the actual feature instances from the matched IDs. Given a target bounding box, the first method finds features that overlap it, while the other method loops through the *n* nearest features in the order of closest to furthest away. In case the target bounding box is not in the required `[xmin, ymin,xmax,ymax]` format, we force it that way:

```
def quick_overlap(self, bbox):
    """
```

```
        Quickly get features whose bbox overlap the specified bbox
via the spatial index.
        """
        if not hasattr(self, "spindex"):
            raise Exception("You need to create the spatial index
before you can use this method")
        # ensure min,min,max,max pattern
        xs = bbox[0],bbox[2]
        ys = bbox[1],bbox[3]
        bbox = [min(xs),min(ys),max(xs),max(ys)]
        # return generator over results
        results = self.spindex.intersection(bbox)
        return (self[id] for id in results)

    def quick_nearest(self, bbox, n=1):
        """
        Quickly get n features whose bbox are nearest the
specified bbox via the spatial index.
        """
        if not hasattr(self, "spindex"):
            raise Exception("You need to create the spatial index
before you can use this method")
        # ensure min,min,max,max pattern
        xs = bbox[0],bbox[2]
        ys = bbox[1],bbox[3]
        bbox = [min(xs),min(ys),max(xs),max(ys)]
        # return generator over results
        results = self.spindex.nearest(bbox, num_results=n)
        return (self[id] for id in results)
```

Loading vector files

So far, we have not defined the routine that actually loads data from a file into our
`VectorData` interface. This is contained in a separate module as `vector/loader.py`.
Start off the module by importing the necessary modules (don't worry if you have
never heard of them before, we will install them shortly):

```
# import builtins
import os

# import fileformat modules
import shapefile as pyshp
import pygeoj
```

The main point of the loader module is to use a function, which we call `from_file()`, that takes a filepath and automatically detects which file type it is. It then loads it with the appropriate routine. Once loaded, it returns the information that our `VectorData` class expects: fieldnames, a list of row lists, a list of GeoJSON dictionaries of the geometries, and CRS information. An optional encoding argument determines the text encoding of the file (which the user will have to know or guess in advance), but more on that later. Go ahead and make it now:

```
def from_file(filepath, encoding="utf8"):

    def decode(value):
        if isinstance(value, str):
            return value.decode(encoding)
        else: return value
```

Shapefile

To deal with the shapefile format, an old but very commonly used vector file format, we use the popular and lightweight **PyShp** library. To install it in the command line just type `C:/Python27/Scripts/pip install pyshp`.

Inside the `from_file` function, we first detect if the file is in the shapefile format and then run our routine for loading it. The routine starts using the PyShp module to get access to the file contents through a `shapereader` object. Using the `shapereader` object, we extract the name (the first item) from each field information tuple, and exclude the first field which is always a deletion flag field. The rows are loaded by looping the `shapereader` object's `iterRecords` method.

Loading geometries is slightly more complicated because we want to perform some additional steps. PyShp, like most packages, can format its geometries as GeoJSON dictionaries via its shape object's `__geo_interface__` property. Now, remember from the earlier *Spatial indexing* section, calculating the individual bounding boxes for each individual feature can be costly. One of the benefits of the shapefile format is that each shape's bounding box is stored as part of the shapefile format. Therefore, we take advantage of the fact that they are already calculated for us and stored as a part of the GeoJSON dictionary that we send to initiate our `VectorData` class. We create a `getgeoj` function that adds the bounding box information to the GeoJSON dictionary if it is available (point shapes for instance, do not have a `bbox` attribute) and use it on each shape that we get from the `shapereader` object's `iterShapes` method.

Next, the shapefile formats have an optional `.prj` file containing projection information, so we also try to read this information if it exists, or default to unprojected WGS84 if not. Finally, we have the function return the loaded fields, rows, geometries, and projection so our data module can use them to build a `VectorData` instance.

Here is the final code:

```
# shapefile
if filepath.endswith(".shp"):
    shapereader = pyshp.Reader(filepath)

    # load fields, rows, and geometries
    fields = [decode(fieldinfo[0]) for fieldinfo in
shapereader.fields[1:]]
    rows = [ [decode(value) for value in record] for record in
shapereader.iterRecords()]
    def getgeoj(obj):
        geoj = obj.__geo_interface__
        if hasattr(obj, "bbox"): geoj["bbox"] = obj.bbox
        return geoj
    geometries = [getgeoj(shape) for shape in
shapereader.iterShapes()]

    # load projection string from .prj file if exists
    if os.path.lexists(filepath[:-4] + ".prj"):
        crs = open(filepath[:-4] + ".prj", "r").read()
    else: crs = "+proj=longlat +ellps=WGS84 +datum=WGS84
+no_defs"

    return fields, rows, geometries, crs
```

GeoJSON

GeoJSON is a more recent file format than the shapefile format, due to its simplicity it is widely used, especially by web applications. The library we will use to read them is PyGeoj, created by the author. To install it, in the command line, type `C:/Python27/Scripts/pip install pygeoj`.

To detect GeoJSON files, there is no rule as to what their filename extension should be, but it tends to be either `.geojson` or just `.json`. We then load the GeoJSON file into a PyGeoj object. The GeoJSON features don't need to have all the same fields, so we use a convenience method that gets only the fieldnames that are common to all features.

Rows are loaded by looping the features and accessing the `properties` attribute. This PyGeoj object's geometries consist purely of GeoJSON dictionaries, same as our own data structure, so we just load the geometries as is. Finally, we return all the loaded information. Refer to the following code:

```
# geojson file
elif filepath.endswith((".geojson",".json")):
    geojfile = pygeoj.load(filepath)

    # load fields, rows, and geometries
    fields = [decode(field) for field in
geojfile.common_attributes]
    rows = [[decode(feat.properties[field]) for field in
fields] for feat in geojfile]
    geometries = [feat.geometry.__geo_interface__ for feat in
geojfile]

    # load projection
    crs = geojfile.crs

    return fields, rows, geometries, crs
```

File format not supported

Since we do not intend to support any additional file formats for now, we add an `else` clause returning an unsupported file format exception if the file path didn't match any of the previous formats:

```
else:
    raise Exception("Could not create vector data from the
given filepath: the filetype extension is either missing or not
supported")
```

Saving vector data

To enable saving our vector data back to the file, create a module called `vector/saver.py`. At the top of the script, we import the necessary modules:

```
# import builtins
import itertools

# import fileformats
import shapefile as pyshp
import pygeoj
```

The main purpose of the saver module is a simple `to_file` function, which will do the saving for us. We do not allow a CRS projection argument, as that will require a way to format projections according to different standards which, to my knowledge, can currently only be done using GDAL, which we opted not to use.

Now, a common difficulty faced when saving files containing text is that you must remember to encode your **Unicode** type text (text with fancy non-English characters) back into machine-readable byte strings, or if they are Python objects such as dates, we want to get their byte-string representation. Therefore, the first thing we do is create a quick function that will do this for us, using the text encoding argument from the `to_file` function. So far, our code looks like this:

```python
def to_file(fields, rows, geometries, filepath, encoding="utf8"):

    def encode(value):
        if isinstance(value, (float,int)):
            # nrs are kept as nrs
            return value
        elif isinstance(value, unicode):
            # unicode is custom encoded into bytestring
            return value.encode(encoding)
        else:
            # brute force anything else to string representation
            return bytes(value)
```

Shapefile

For saving vector data to the shapefile format, once we have created a `shapewriter` object, we first want to detect and set all the fields with the correct value types. Instead of dealing with potential type mismatches, we just check whether all valid values in each field are numeric, and if not, we force to text type. In the end, we assign to each field, a field tuple with a cleaned and encoded fieldname (shapefiles do not allow names longer than 10 characters or that contain spaces), the value type (where *C* stands for text characters and *N* for numbers), the maximum text length, and the decimal precision for numbers.

Once this is done, we can start writing our file. Unfortunately, PyShp currently has no ready-made way to save geometries directly from GeoJSON dictionaries, so we first create a function to do this conversion. Doing this requires making an empty PyShp shape instance and setting the correct `shapeType` property. The `points` attribute is a continuous list of all coordinate points, which for multigeometries is separated at the index positions indicated in the `parts` attribute.

We can then loop all our features, use our function to convert GeoJSON into PyShp shape instances, append those to the writer's _shapes list, encode and add the feature's row with the `record` method, and finish up by saving. The entire code is shown as follows:

```
# shapefile
if filepath.endswith(".shp"):
    shapewriter = pyshp.Writer()

    # set fields with correct fieldtype
    for fieldindex,fieldname in enumerate(fields):
        for row in rows:
            value = row[fieldindex]
            if value != "":
                try:
                    # make nr fieldtype if content can be made
into nr
                    float(value)
                    fieldtype = "N"
                    fieldlen = 16
                    decimals = 8
                except:
                    # but turn to text if any of the cells
cannot be made to float bc they are txt
                    fieldtype = "C"
                    fieldlen = 250
                    decimals = 0
                break
            else:
                # empty value, so just keep assuming nr type
                fieldtype = "N"
                fieldlen = 16
                decimals = 8
        # clean fieldname
        fieldname = fieldname.replace(" ","_")[:10]
        # write field
        shapewriter.field(fieldname.encode(encoding),
fieldtype, fieldlen, decimals)

    # convert geojson to shape
    def geoj2shape(geoj):
        # create empty pyshp shape
        shape = pyshp._Shape()
        # set shapetype
```

```
geojtype = geoj["type"]
if geojtype == "Null":
    pyshptype = pyshp.NULL
elif geojtype == "Point":
    pyshptype = pyshp.POINT
elif geojtype == "LineString":
    pyshptype = pyshp.POLYLINE
elif geojtype == "Polygon":
    pyshptype = pyshp.POLYGON
elif geojtype == "MultiPoint":
    pyshptype = pyshp.MULTIPOINT
elif geojtype == "MultiLineString":
    pyshptype = pyshp.POLYLINE
elif geojtype == "MultiPolygon":
    pyshptype = pyshp.POLYGON
shape.shapeType = pyshptype

# set points and parts
if geojtype == "Point":
    shape.points = [ geoj["coordinates"] ]
    shape.parts = [0]
elif geojtype in ("MultiPoint","LineString"):
    shape.points = geoj["coordinates"]
    shape.parts = [0]
elif geojtype in ("Polygon"):
    points = []
    parts = []
    index = 0
    for ext_or_hole in geoj["coordinates"]:
        points.extend(ext_or_hole)
        parts.append(index)
        index += len(ext_or_hole)
    shape.points = points
    shape.parts = parts
elif geojtype in ("MultiLineString"):
    points = []
    parts = []
    index = 0
    for linestring in geoj["coordinates"]:
        points.extend(linestring)
        parts.append(index)
        index += len(linestring)
    shape.points = points
```

```
            shape.parts = parts
        elif geojtype in ("MultiPolygon"):
            points = []
            parts = []
            index = 0
            for polygon in geoj["coordinates"]:
                for ext_or_hole in polygon:
                    points.extend(ext_or_hole)
                    parts.append(index)
                    index += len(ext_or_hole)
            shape.points = points
            shape.parts = parts
        return shape

    # iterate through original shapes
    for row,geom in itertools.izip(rows, geometries):
        shape = geoj2shape(geom)
        shapewriter._shapes.append(shape)
        shapewriter.record(*[encode(value) for value in row])

    # save
    shapewriter.save(filepath)
```

GeoJSON

Saving GeoJSON is slightly more straightforward to implement with the PyGeoj package. We start by creating a new `geojwriter` object, following which we loop all of our features, encode Unicode text to byte strings, add them to the `geojwriter` instance, and save once finished:

```
# GeoJSON file
elif filepath.endswith((".geojson",".json")):
    geojwriter = pygeoj.new()
    for row,geom in itertools.izip(rows,geometries):
        # encode row values
        row = (encode(value) for value in row)
        rowdict = dict(zip(fields, row))
        # add feature
        geojwriter.add_feature(properties=rowdict,
                               geometry=geom)

    # save
    geojwriter.save(filepath)
```

File format not supported

Finally, we add an `else` clause to provide a message that the user attempted to save to a file format, for which saving is not yet supported:

```
else:
        raise Exception("Could not save the vector data to the
given filepath: the filetype extension is either missing or not
supported")
```

Raster data

Now that we have implemented a data structure for loading and saving vector data, we can proceed to do the same for raster data. As stated earlier, we will be creating three submodules inside our `raster` package: `data`, `loader`, and `saver`. To make these accessible from their parent raster package, we need to import it in `raster/__init__.py` as follows:

```
from . import data
from . import loader
from . import saver
```

A data interface for raster data

Raster data has a very different structure that we must accommodate, and we begin by making its data interface. The code for this interface will be contained in a module of its own inside the raster folder. To create this module now, save it as `raster/data.py`. Start it out with a few basic imports, including the loader and saver modules that we have not yet created and PIL which we installed in *Chapter 1, Preparing to Build Your Own GIS Application*:

```
# import builtins
import sys, os, itertools, operator

# import internals
from . import loader
from . import saver

# import PIL as the data container
import PIL.Image, PIL.ImageMath
```

The raster data structure

A raster consists of one or more grids of data referred to as **bands**. These grids and the values in each of their **cells** represent how a piece of information flows across space-like pixels in a photograph:

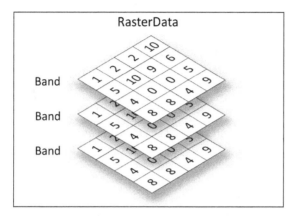

Given raster data's similarities with imagery data, we take advantage of our existing PIL imaging library that we imported earlier and use it for our application's raster data structure. Its C-based code makes it fast and memory-efficient, and it already contains a lot of the pixel-based raster functionality that we want to be able to do eventually.

At the top level, our RasterData class contains some raster metadata and one or more **Band** layers, which are just wrappers around pixel image data containers. When creating a new RasterData class, we usually load from a file path. The actual loading is outsourced to a loader module we create later, which returns a dictionary of various metadata about the raster (info), a list of one or more bands (bands), and the definition of its coordinate reference system (crs). We can also create a new RasterData class from non-spatial data based on a list of lists representing a grid or an ordinary image file, in which case it is up to us to define its CRS and geospatial metadata (we return to this shortly).

The Band class is where the actual values are stored. We keep one reference to a PIL image (img) so that we can use its various imagery processing methods, and one reference to the image's pixel access object (cells) so we can tinker directly with individual pixels. Each pixel is accessed as a Cell class instance, which provides a convenience method for its row/column position.

Look at the following code:

```
class Cell:
    def __init__(self, band, col, row):
        self.band = band
        self.col, self.row = col, row

    def __repr__(self):
        return "Cell(col=%s, row=%s, value=%s)" %(self.col,
self.row, self.value)

    @property
    def value(self):
        return self.band.cells[self.col, self.row]


class Band:
    def __init__(self, img, cells):
        self.img = img
        self.cells = cells

    def __iter__(self):
        width,height = self.img.size
        for row in range(height):
            for col in range(width):
                yield Cell(self, col, row)

    def get(self, col, row):
        return Cell(self, col, row)

    def set(self, col, row, value):
        self.cells[col,row] = value

    def copy(self):
        img = self.img.copy()
        cells = img.load()
        return Band(img, cells)


class RasterData:
    def __init__(self, filepath=None, data=None, image=None,
**kwargs):
```

```
        self.filepath = filepath

        if filepath:
            info, bands, crs = loader.from_file(filepath)
        elif data:
            info, bands, crs = loader.from_lists(data, **kwargs)
        elif image:
            info, bands, crs = loader.from_image(image, **kwargs)
        else:
            info, bands, crs = loader.new(**kwargs)

        self.bands = [Band(img,cells) for img,cells in bands]

        self.info = info

        self.crs = crs

        self.update_geotransform()

    def __iter__(self):
        for band in self.bands:
            yield band

    @property
    def width(self):
        return self.bands[0].img.size[0]

    @property
    def height(self):
        return self.bands[0].img.size[1]

    def copy(self):
        new = RasterData(width=self.width, height=self.height,
    **self.info)
        new.bands = [band.copy() for band in self.bands]
        new._cached_mask = self.mask
        return new
```

Positioning the raster in coordinate space

We are not done yet. While the gridded structure of our raster bands gives us a sense of the relative location of each value within the grid, it does not say anything about their real-world geographical position in the same way that a Feature geometry's coordinates does. This is why we need additional geospatial metadata about the raster. To position our values in geographic space, there are two ways this can be specified in our `info` metadata dictionary:

- We need to translate one of the cells (`xy_cell`) to a geographic or projected coordinate (`xy_geo`) and specify the coordinate width and height of its cells (`cellwidth` and `cellheight`) so that we can move and resize the raster. These are essentially just components of the transform coefficients described next.

- In some cases, such as aerial imagery taken along some arbitrary direction, it might not be enough to move and resize the raster. We may also need to rotate and possibly skew the raster. To do this, we need a set of affine transform coefficients (`transform_ceoffs`), so we can recalculate the position of each and every cell to end up with the warped image. This is also known as a **geotransform**.

 There is also a third possibility, by using a sample of geocoded points, which can then be approximated using a non-linear transformation, but we do not cover this method. For more on positioning rasters in coordinate space, check out: http://www.remotesensing.org/geotiff/spec/geotiff2.6.html.

The following diagram illustrates how a set of geotransform coefficients might offset, scale, and rotate a raster dataset to position it in coordinate space, which usually requires flipping the *y* axis:

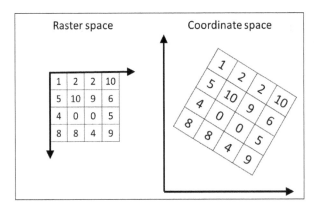

One last aspect of raster data that should be considered is where in each cell the coordinate offsets are anchored; either at the cell center or any of its four corners. We store this information as xy_anchor. However, as the difference is very small, we choose not to do anything with it for our simple application.

Based on the provided geospatial metadata, we must first calculate the regular and inverse transform coefficients (update_geotransform()) so that we can map back and forth between cell positions and spatial coordinates (cell_to_geo() and geo_to_cell()). With this foundation, we can get further information about the bounding box of the raster (bbox). Most importantly, we allow repositioning/warping the raster (and its nodata mask that we create later) into a new raster that reflects its real-world location within a specified bounding box and at a specified width/height resolution (positioned()). This repositioning is easy to implement by transforming from the old to the new coordinate bounding box using PIL's quad transform. Let's add these functionalities to the RasterData structure:

```
    def cell_to_geo(self, column, row):
        [xscale, xskew, xoffset, yskew, yscale, yoffset] =
self.transform_coeffs
        x, y = column, row
        x_coord = x*xscale + y*xskew + xoffset
        y_coord = x*yskew + y*yscale + yoffset
        return x_coord, y_coord

    def geo_to_cell(self, x, y, fraction=False):
        [xscale, xskew, xoffset, yskew, yscale, yoffset] =
self.inv_transform_coeffs
        column = x*xscale + y*xskew + xoffset
        row = x*yskew + y*yscale + yoffset
        if not fraction:
            # round to nearest cell
            column,row = int(round(column)), int(round(row))
        return column,row

    @property
    def bbox(self):
        # get corner coordinates of raster
        xleft_coord,ytop_coord = self.cell_to_geo(0,0)
        xright_coord,ybottom_coord = self.cell_to_geo(self.width,
self.height)
        return [xleft_coord,ytop_coord,xright_coord,ybottom_coord]

    def update_geotransform(self):
```

```
        info = self.info

        # get coefficients needed to convert from raster to
geographic space
        if info.get("transform_coeffs"):
            [xscale, xskew, xoffset,
             yskew, yscale, yoffset] = info["transform_coeffs"]
        else:
            xcell,ycell = info["xy_cell"]
            xgeo,ygeo = info["xy_geo"]
            xoffset,yoffset = xgeo - xcell, ygeo - ycell
            xscale,yscale = info["cellwidth"], info["cellheight"]
            xskew,yskew = 0,0
        self.transform_coeffs = [xscale, xskew, xoffset, yskew,
yscale, yoffset]

        # and the inverse coefficients to go from geographic space
to raster
        # taken from Sean Gillies' "affine.py"
        a,b,c,d,e,f = self.transform_coeffs
        det = a*e - b*d
        if det != 0:
            idet = 1 / float(det)
            ra = e * idet
            rb = -b * idet
            rd = -d * idet
            re = a * idet
            a,b,c,d,e,f = (ra, rb, -c*ra - f*rb,
                           rd, re, -c*rd - f*re)
            self.inv_transform_coeffs = a,b,c,d,e,f
        else:
            raise Exception("Error with the transform matrix, \
                            a raster should not collapse upon
itself")

    def positioned(self, width, height, coordspace_bbox):
        # GET COORDS OF ALL 4 VIEW SCREEN CORNERS
        xleft,ytop,xright,ybottom = coordspace_bbox
        viewcorners = [(xleft,ytop), (xleft,ybottom),
(xright,ybottom), (xright,ytop)]

        # FIND PIXEL LOCS OF ALL THESE COORDS ON THE RASTER
        viewcorners_pixels = [self.geo_to_cell(*point,
fraction=True) for point in viewcorners]
```

```
        # ON RASTER, PERFORM QUAD TRANSFORM
        #(FROM VIEW SCREEN COORD CORNERS IN PIXELS TO RASTER COORD
CORNERS IN PIXELS)
        flattened = [xory for point in viewcorners_pixels for xory
in point]
        newraster = self.copy()

        #self.update_mask()
        mask = self.mask

        # make mask over
        masktrans = mask.transform((width,height), PIL.Image.QUAD,
                        flattened, resample=PIL.Image.NEAREST)

        for band in newraster.bands:
            datatrans = band.img.transform((width,height),
PIL.Image.QUAD,
                                flattened,
resample=PIL.Image.NEAREST)
            trans = PIL.Image.new(datatrans.mode, datatrans.size)
            trans.paste(datatrans, (0,0), masktrans)
            # store image and cells
            band.img = trans
            band.cells = band.img.load()

        return newraster,masktrans
```

Nodata masking

Sometimes cells in a raster contain missing data, so each `RasterData` class will define a `nodata_value` in its `info` metadata dictionary if specified. This is important because these `nodata` cells have to be ignored while visualizing or performing operations. Therefore, in our data interface, we need to create an additional image grid that knows the location of missing values so that we can use it with PIL to mask or hide away those values. This mask is accessed as a dynamic property that we cache for repeated use. Refer to the following code:

```
    @property
    def mask(self):
        if hasattr(self, "_cached_mask"):
            return self._cached_mask

        else:
            nodata = self.info.get("nodata_value")
            if nodata != None:
```

```
                    # mask out nodata
                if self.bands[0].img.mode in ("F","I"):
                        # if 32bit float or int values, need to
manually check each cell
                    mask = PIL.Image.new("1", (self.width,
self.height), 1)
                    px = mask.load()
                    for col in xrange(self.width):
                        for row in xrange(self.height):
                            value = (band.cells[col,row] for band
in self.bands)
                            # mask out only where all bands have
nodata value
                            if all((val == nodata for val in
value)):
                                px[col,row] = 0
                else:
                    # use the much faster point method
                    masks = []
                    for band in self.bands:
                        mask = band.img.point(lambda px: 1 if px
!= nodata else 0, "1")
                        masks.append(mask)
                    # mask out where all bands have nodata value
                    masks_namedict = dict([("mask%i"%i, mask) for
i,mask in enumerate(masks) ])
                    expr = " & ".join(masks_namedict.keys())
                    mask = PIL.ImageMath.eval(expr,
**masks_namedict).convert("1")
            else:
                # EVEN IF NO NODATA, NEED TO CREATE ORIGINAL MASK,
                # TO PREVENT INFINITE OUTSIDE BORDER AFTER
GEOTRANSFORM
                nodata = 0
                mask = PIL.Image.new("1", self.bands[0].img.size,
1)
            self._cached_mask = mask
            return self._cached_mask
```

Loading raster data

Now, it is time to add the loading to the `Raster` class. Unfortunately, besides GDAL, there are not many independent file format libraries that focus on loading geographic raster formats. Nevertheless, we are still able to make a minimal loader of the common GeoTIFF file format based on PIL. We initiate the module with some imports and save it as `raster/loader.py`:

```
# import internals
import sys, os, itertools, operator
# import PIL as the image loader
import PIL.Image
```

The main purpose of our loader module is to provide a `from_file` function that returns the necessary pieces to our raster data structure. Before we get into loading each raster file format, we begin with a function to read metadata from the ESRI world file format that sometimes accompany raster files. The world file is a very simple text file containing six values defining the affine geotransform metadata discussed previously, and its filename extension is either `.wld` or a variation on the image file type it accompanies.

With support for this world file, we can easily allow the loading and saving of image-like raster formats with PIL, such as `.png`, `.bmp`, `.gif`, or `.jpg`, but we do not do so in this book. The world file also sometimes comes with the ESRI ASCII raster format, a simple text file format, that is easy to understand and implement.

Take a look at the following code:

```
def from_file(filepath):

    def check_world_file(filepath):
        worldfilepath = None

        # try to find worldfile
        dir, filename_and_ext = os.path.split(filepath)
        filename, extension = os.path.splitext(filename_and_ext)
        dir_and_filename = os.path.join(dir, filename)

        # first check generic .wld extension
        if os.path.lexists(dir_and_filename + ".wld"):
            worldfilepath = dir_and_filename + ".wld"

        # if not, check filetype-specific world file extensions
        else:
            # get filetype-specific world file extension
            if extension in ("tif","tiff","geotiff"):
                extension = ".tfw"
            else:
                return None
            # check if exists
            if os.path.lexists(dir_and_filename + extension):
                worldfilepath = dir_and_filename + extension
```

```
            # then return contents if file found
        if worldfilepath:
            with open(worldfilepath) as worldfile:
                # note that the params are arranged slightly
differently
                # ...in the world file from the usual affine
a,b,c,d,e,f
                # ...so remember to rearrange their sequence later
                xscale,yskew,xskew,yscale,xoff,yoff =
worldfile.read().split()
            return [xscale,yskew,xskew,yscale,xoff,yoff]
```

GeoTIFF

GeoTIFF is a geographic extension of the flexible TIFF image file format, with the only difference being additional geo-specific metadata tags. PIL can read TIFF files along with their metadata tags, but once we fully load or access the image contents, PIL makes it format-neutral by stripping away any format-specific info. Therefore, you must extract the geo tags before you do anything with the image. Once extracted, it is up to us to interpret the tag codes, because PIL does not know about the GeoTIFF specification. We extract tags relating to the geotransform, nodata value, and the name and text-encoded tags of the CRS (there are numerous other CRS-specific tags, but it will be too much to deal with all of them here). Finally, we split the image into its individual bands in case it is a composite RGB raster, and return the info metadata, band tuples, and CRS.

 The full-GeoTIFF specification can be found online at http://www.remotesensing.org/geotiff/spec/contents.html.

Refer to the following code:

```
    elif filepath.lower().endswith((".tif",".tiff",".geotiff")):
        main_img = PIL.Image.open(filepath)
        raw_tags = dict(main_img.tag.items())

        def process_metadata(raw_tags):
            # check tag definitions here
            info = dict()
            if raw_tags.has_key(1025):
                # GTRasterTypeGeoKey, aka midpoint pixels vs
topleft area pixels
                if raw_tags.get(1025) == (1,):
                    # is area
```

```
                    info["cell_anchor"] = "center"
                elif raw_tags.get(1025) == (2,):
                    # is point
                    info["cell_anchor"] = "nw"
            if raw_tags.has_key(34264):
                # ModelTransformationTag, aka 4x4 transform
coeffs...
                a,b,c,d,
                e,f,g,h,
                i,j,k,l,
                m,n,o,p = raw_tags.get(34264)
                # But we don't want to meddle with 3-D transforms,
                # ...so for now only get the 2-D affine parameters
                xscale,xskew,xoff = a,b,d
                yskew,yscale,yoff = e,f,h
                info["transform_coeffs"] =
xscale,xskew,xoff,yskew,yscale,yoff
            else:
                if raw_tags.has_key(33922):
                    # ModelTiepointTag
                    x, y, z, geo_x, geo_y, geo_z =
raw_tags.get(33922)
                    info["xy_cell"] = x,y
                    info["xy_geo"] = geo_x,geo_y
                if raw_tags.has_key(33550):
                    # ModelPixelScaleTag
                    scalex,scaley,scalez = raw_tags.get(33550)
                    info["cellwidth"] = scalex
                    info["cellheight"] = -scaley # note:
cellheight must be inversed because geotiff has a reversed y-
axis (ie 0,0 is in upperleft corner)
            if raw_tags.get(42113):
                info["nodata_value"] = eval(raw_tags.get(42113)) #
eval from string to nr
            return info

        def read_crs(raw_tags):
            crs = dict()
            if raw_tags.get(34735):
                # GeoKeyDirectoryTag
                crs["proj_params"] = raw_tags.get(34735)
            if raw_tags.get(34737):
                # GeoAsciiParamsTag
                crs["proj_name"] = raw_tags.get(34737)
```

```
            return crs

        # read geotiff metadata tags
        info = process_metadata(raw_tags)

        # if no geotiff tag info look for world file transform
coefficients
        if len(info) <= 1 and not info.get("transform_coeffs"):
            transform_coeffs = check_world_file(filepath)
            if transform_coeffs:
                # rearrange the world file param sequence to match
affine transform
                [xscale,yskew,xskew,yscale,xoff,yoff] =
transform_coeffs
                info["transform_coeffs"] =
[xscale,xskew,xoff,yskew,yscale,yoff]
            else:
                raise Exception("Couldn't find any geotiff tags or
world file needed to position the image in space")

        # group image bands and pixel access into band tuples
        bands = []
        for img in main_img.split():
            cells = img.load()
            bands.append((img,cells))

        # read coordinate ref system
        crs = read_crs(raw_tags)

        return info, bands, crs
```

File format not supported

As with the vector loader, we raise an exception if an attempt to load an unsupported raster file format has been made, using the following code:

```
    else:
        raise Exception("Could not create a raster from the given
filepath: the filetype extension is either missing or not
supported")
```

Saving raster data

Finally, we want to save our raster data back to file, so we create a new module called `raster/saver.py`. We start out with some imports as follows:

```
# import builtins
Import os

# import PIL as the saver
import PIL
import PIL.TiffImagePlugin
import PIL.TiffTags
```

Inside the main `to_file` function, we define a cross-format function to combine raster bands into a final image ready to be saved, and a basic method for creating the `worldfile` containing geotransform:

```
def to_file(bands, info, filepath):
    def combine_bands(bands):
        # saving in image-like format, so combine and prep final
image
        if len(bands) == 1:
            img = bands[0].img
            return img
        elif len(bands) == 3:
            # merge all images together
            mode = "RGB"
            bands = [band.img for band in bands]
            img = PIL.Image.merge(mode, bands)
            return img
        elif len(bands) == 4:
            # merge all images together
            mode - "RGBA"
            bands = [band.img for band in bands]
            img = PIL.Image.merge(mode, bands)
            return img
        else:
            # raise error if more than 4 bands, because PIL cannot
save such images
            raise Exception("Cannot save more than 4 bands to one
file; split and save each band separately")

    def create_world_file(savepath, geotrans):
        dir, filename_and_ext = os.path.split(savepath)
        filename, extension = os.path.splitext(filename_and_ext)
```

```
        world_file_path = os.path.join(dir, filename) + ".wld"
        with open(world_file_path, "w") as writer:
            # rearrange transform coefficients and write
            xscale,xskew,xoff,yskew,yscale,yoff = geotrans
            writer.writelines([xscale, yskew, xskew, yscale, xoff,
yoff])
```

GeoTIFF

Next, we allow saving to GeoTIFF using PIL. Until recently, saving GeoTIFF with PIL was not possible. This was because PIL had not implemented saving TIFF tags of type `float` or `double`, this would lead to errors because most GeoTIFF tags are double values. A recent user contribution added the required support for double tags, and by the time you read this, PIL's Pillow fork should have hopefully incremented to a new stable version 2.8.2.

If Pillow is still on version 2.8.1, you will have to add this support yourself by modifying your PIL package in `site-packages`. After opening PIL's `TiffImagePlugin.py` file, you will see that the `ImageFileDirectory` class has a `save` method starting at around line 483. This method loops through all the provided tags with several `if` statements checking for different tag value types. Between the `if` statements commented as `untyped data` and `string data`, you must add a new `if` statement with the following code for floats and doubles, and remember to save your changes:

```
elif typ in (11, 12):
    # float value
    tmap = {11: 'f', 12: 'd'}
    if not isinstance(value, tuple):
        value = (value,)
    a = array.array(tmap[typ], value)
    if self.prefix != native_prefix:
        a.byteswap()
    data = a.tostring()
```

The actual saving procedure is implemented by leveraging some less well-known features of PIL. In order to save our raster's metadata as tags in the file itself, we must refer to PIL's `TiffImagePlugin` module, disable its use of the LibTIFF library, and create an empty `ImageFileDirectory` class to hold the tags. Each added tag value is set by index setting the tag container and must be followed by index setting the tag value type on the container's `tagtype` property.

Once all the geotransform, nodata, and projection tags are set, we simply combine the band images into one and pass the tag container as an extra argument to the final save() call:

```python
        elif filepath.endswith((".tif", ".tiff", ".geotiff")):
            # write directly to tag info
            PIL.TiffImagePlugin.WRITE_LIBTIFF = False
            tags = PIL.TiffImagePlugin.ImageFileDirectory()
            if info.get("cell_anchor"):
                # GTRasterTypeGeoKey, aka midpoint pixels vs topleft
area pixels
                if info.get("cell_anchor") == "center":
                    # is area
                    tags[1025] = 1.0
                    tags.tagtype[1025] = 12 #double, only works with
PIL patch
                elif info.get("cell_anchor") == "nw":
                    # is point
                    tags[1025] = 2.0
                    tags.tagtype[1025] = 12 #double, only works with
PIL patch
            if info.get("transform_coeffs"):
                # ModelTransformationTag, aka 4x4 transform coeffs...
                tags[34264] =
tuple(map(float,info.get("transform_coeffs")))
                tags.tagtype[34264] = 12 #double, only works with PIL
patch
            else:
                if info.get("xy_cell") and info.get("xy_geo"):
                    # ModelTiepointTag
                    x,y = info["xy_cell"]
                    geo_x,geo_y = info["xy_geo"]
                    tags[33922] =
tuple(map(float, [x,y,0,geo_x,geo_y,0]))
                    tags.tagtype[33922] = 12 #double, only works with
  PIL patch
                if info.get("cellwidth") and info.get("cellheight"):
                    # ModelPixelScaleTag
                    scalex,scaley =
info["cellwidth"],info["cellheight"]
                    tags[33550] = tuple(map(float, [scalex,scaley,0]))
                    tags.tagtype[33550] = 12 #double, only works with
PIL patch
            if info.get("nodata_value"):
```

```
        tags[42113] = bytes(info.get("nodata_value"))
        tags.tagtype[42113] = 2 #ascii

    # finally save the file using tiffinfo headers
    img = combine_bands(bands)
    img.save(filepath, tiffinfo=tags)
```

File format not supported

These are the only raster file formats we allow saving to for now:

```
else:
        raise Exception("Could not save the raster to the given
filepath: the filetype extension is either missing or not
supported")
```

Summary

In this chapter, we built the core foundation of our application. In each of our `vector` and `raster` folders, we created three new modules that allow us to access, edit, and share some popular geographic data formats. Our folder structure should, therefore, look something like this:

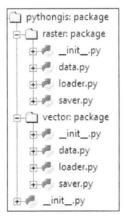

This is the minimum we will need for any type of GIS application. We can theoretically, at this point, make a minimalistic application focused only on loading and handling file formats. In the next chapter, we jump straight into making the visual interface application, so we can have a real interactive application up and running as soon as possible.

3
Designing the Visual Look of Our Application

We have now come to the part where we want to design how our application will look and feel. For this **graphical user interface (GUI)**, we take the path of least resistance and go with the **Tkinter** library since this is a standard built-in library in the official Python installations, at least for Windows and Mac. Other reasons for choosing Tkinter is that it is fairly easy to use and is slightly more Pythonic than some of the newer third-party GUI libraries.

If you have not used Tkinter before, you should still be able to follow along. The basic idea of Tkinter is that you create widget classes for each graphical element of your GUI, defining their look and placement. Complex elements can be created by nesting widgets within widgets. You can also bind functions to user interaction events.

 To learn more about Tkinter, I highly recommend using John W. Shipman's reference guide, available from http://infohost. nmt.edu/tcc/help/pubs/tkinter/tkinter.pdf.

In this chapter you will:

- Set up the general code structure to make a themed and highly customizable GIS application
- Create a toolbox of specialized user interface widgets that can connect to our underlying GIS functionality
- Use this toolbox of widgets to glue together the visual design and layout of our application
- Learn how to test run our application

Setting up the GUI package

We begin the chapter by setting up the structural skeleton for our application GUI. This should be logically separate from the rest of our code so we give it a subpackage of its own. Inside the top level `pythongis` folder, create a package folder called `app` with an `__init__.py` file inside it. Have it import the rest of the modules we will be creating:

```
from . import builder
from . import dialogues
from . import toolkit
from . import icons
```

To make our `app` package accessible from our top level `pythongis` package, we similarly need to import it in `pythongis/__init__.py` as follows:

```
from . import app
```

The purpose of the `app` package is that we should be able to define how our GUI looks and behaves, and with a single line of code, `pythongis.app.run()`, we should be able to invoke it. The actual definition and layout of our GUI should be contained in a module we call `app/builder.py` (which we return to at the end of the chapter). The builder in turn relies on a set of predefined GUI building blocks, which we define in a subpackage folder called `app/toolkit`. This toolkit's `__init__.py` file imports the building block modules that we are going to create throughout the chapter:

```
from .buttons import *
from .layers import *
from .map import *
from .popups import *
from .ribbon import *
from .statusbar import *
from .toolbars import *

from . import theme
from . import dispatch
```

In addition to our builder and toolkit, we also need an `app/dialogues.py` module that defines application-specific dialogue windows.

Last but not least, an important part of an application structure is how to access icons and images. To make our icons readily available to any widget that may need them, we create an app/icons package. This package folder is where we will save all our icons. When an application widget needs an icon, it simply asks the icons package for the icon name and size via get() and in return receives a Tkinter compatible PhotoImage object. Create its __init__.py file now:

```python
import os
import PIL.Image, PIL.ImageTk

ICONSFOLDER = os.path.split(__file__)[0]

def get(iconname, width=None, height=None):
    iconpath = os.path.join(ICONSFOLDER, iconname)

    if os.path.lexists(iconpath):
        img = PIL.Image.open(iconpath)
        if width or height:
            width = width or img.size[0]
            height = height or img.size[1]
            img = img.resize((width,height), PIL.Image.ANTIALIAS)
        tk_img = PIL.ImageTk.PhotoImage(img)
        return tk_img

    else:
        raise Exception("No icon by that name")
```

Once you created all of these, we should be ready to go. Your app folder structure should look like this:

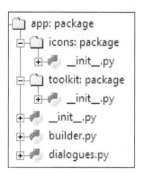

Creating the toolkit building blocks

Before we can start designing our GUI layout, we have to create the `toolkit` package containing the underlying building blocks or design elements that we will be using. Tkinter already provides a set of basic GUI element or **widget** classes, such as `Buttons`, `Labels`, or `CheckBoxes`, with methods for placing them in the application window or nested within each other. To stay consistent with this logic, we subclass these Tkinter widgets and expand on them to make our own specialized building block widgets. This way our GUI code becomes consistent, stable, and reusable.

In our `toolkit` package, we want to have a few widgets readily available: icon buttons, toolbars, a ribbon tab system, a status bar, a panel overview to contain data layers, a map widget, and pop-up window templates. We also need a way for our buttons to connect with and execute geospatial work tasks from our GIS code library, so we make a command dispatch tool. However, before we start making widgets, let's set up an easy way to style them.

Themed styling

To give our application a sense of style, we have to define things like background color or text font in each and every one of our toolkit widgets. To make this styling more flexible, we centralize the styling instructions into a separate module which we call `app/toolkit/theme.py`. The various widgets can then import the styling instructions from this theme module, which can be easily changed and modified as we develop our application, or perhaps even as a customizable feature by the end user.

When specifying colors in Tkinter, you can either specify hex color strings or names of colors predefined by Tkinter. Let's make the main background color of our application a light grey, with five different shades all the way up until pure white. We also want some more unique colors for highlighting purposes, one with two shades of orange, and an alternative one with two shades of blue:

```
color1 = "Grey69"
color2 = "Grey79"
color3 = "Grey89"
color4 = "Grey99"
color5 = "white"

strongcolor1 = "gold"
strongcolor2 = "dark orange"

alterncolor1 = "DodgerBlue"
alterncolor2 = "Blue3"
```

For the full list of valid Tkinter color names and their appearance, see `http://wiki.tcl.tk/37701`.

The type and size of font one uses is also a crucial part of application design, so we decide to use the trendy Segoe font used in Windows 8. Tkinter fonts can be specified with a tuple containing the font name, size, and optionally the type of emphasis. We create two main shades of text fonts, one normal and one weaker one for less important background text. We also create two types of title/header text fonts for extra emphasis, one normal and one white, in case we need to display text on darker backgrounds:

```
titlefont1 = {"type": ("Segoe UI", 12, "bold"),
              "color": "black"}
titlefont1_contrast = {"type": ("Segoe UI", 12, "bold"),
              "color": "white"}

font1 = {"type": ("Segoe UI", 10),
         "color": "black"}
font2 = {"type": ("Segoe UI", 10),
         "color": "Grey42"}
```

Basic buttons

Now, we can begin making widgets. Although Tkinter already comes with **Button** widgets, we will create some of our own so that each button we create is already styled in the way that we want, and we can simplify the process of giving them icons. Therefore, we create our first module which we call `app/toolkit/buttons.py` in the `toolkit` package. At the top, we import some necessary things:

```
# Import builtins
import sys, os

# Import GUI libraries
import Tkinter as tk
from tkFileDialog import askopenfilenames, asksaveasfilename
import PIL, PIL.Image, PIL.ImageTk

# Import internals
from .. import icons
```

Next, we import our theme module and define the style we will use for buttons as dictionary entries. Under normal circumstances we want buttons to have a light background color with a flat relief. Once the mouse pointer hovers over the button, it *lights up* with a highlight color that turns into an even stronger color if clicked on:

```
# Import theme
from . import theme
style_button_normal = {"fg": theme.font1["color"],
                "font": theme.font1["type"],
                "bg": theme.color4,
                 "relief": "flat",
                 "activebackground": theme.strongcolor2
                 }
style_button_mouseover = {"bg": theme.strongcolor1
                }
```

To implement a Button widget that follows this style, we make a Button widget that subclasses the standard Tkinter button and takes our readily formatted style dictionary as keyword arguments. We also define that it should light up as defined in our hover-dictionary every time the mouse passes over the button:

```
class Button(tk.Button):
    def __init__(self, master, **kwargs):
        # get theme style
        style = style_button_normal.copy()
        style.update(kwargs)

        # initialize
        tk.Button.__init__(self, master, **style)

        # bind event behavior
        def mouse_in(event):
            event.widget.config(style_button_mouseover)
        def mouse_out(event):
            event.widget.config(style_button_normal)

        self.bind("<Enter>", mouse_in)
        self.bind("<Leave>", mouse_out)
```

We also add some commonly needed buttons, such as an **Ok** button with an *Enter/Return* keyboard shortcut that runs a specified function when activated:

```
class OkButton(Button):
    def __init__(self, master, **kwargs):
        # initialize
```

```
if kwargs.get("text") == None:
    kwargs["text"] = "OK"
okfunc = kwargs.get("command")
Button.__init__(self, master, **kwargs)

# bind enter keypress to command function
def runfunc(event):
    okfunc()
self.winfo_toplevel().bind("<Return>", runfunc)
```

Buttons with icons

In our application, we want to illustrate what our buttons do by using small icon images, but as you will soon see, giving icons to buttons in Tkinter requires several custom steps that can quickly become a dull task. Therefore, we create a specialized icon button that does these steps for us.

To create the `IconButton` class, we take our styled button class as the starting point, and all we have to do is add a `set_icon` method. This method retrieves the image via the `icons` package with a size that fits the button, styles the way the image is placed inside the button, assigns it, and stores it as one of the button's attributes so it doesn't get garbage collected.

```
class IconButton(Button):
    def __init__(self, master, **kwargs):
        # initialize
        Button.__init__(self, master, **kwargs)

    def set_icon(self, iconname, **kwargs):
        # get icon as tkinter photoimage, with an optional resize
        tk_img = icons.get(iconname,
                           width=kwargs.get("width"),
                           height=kwargs.get("height"))
        self.config(image=tk_img, **kwargs)
        # resize button to have room for text if compound type
        if not kwargs.get("anchor"): kwargs["anchor"] = "center"
        if kwargs.get("compound"):
            def expand():
                self["width"] += tk_img.width()
                self["height"] += tk_img.height() / 2
            self.after(100, expand)
        # store as attribute, so it doesn't get garbage collected
        self.tk_img = tk_img
```

Toolbars

Buttons should not just be placed randomly around. Instead, we want to group together sets of logically related buttons into areas known as **toolbars**. We create the app/toolkit/toolbars.py module and start it off with the necessary imports and style setting:

```
# Import GUI
import Tkinter as tk

# Import internals
from .buttons import *
from .popups import *

# Import style
from . import theme
style_toolbar_normal = {"bg": theme.color4}
style_namelabel_normal = {"bg": theme.color4,
                          "font": theme.font2["type"],
                          "fg": theme.font2["color"],
                          "pady": 0}
```

The toolbar area is itself a subclass of the Tkinter frame and will consist of a frame area into which buttons will be packed side by side, and a text area on the bottom specifying the purpose of the toolbar. For now, we just create the generic Toolbar class with a convenient add_button method so we can later build and populate specialized toolbars by subclassing this one:

```
class Toolbar(tk.Frame):
    """
    Base class for all toolbars.
    """
    def __init__(self, master, toolbarname, **kwargs):
        # get theme style
        style = style_toolbar_normal.copy()
        style.update(kwargs)

        # Make this class a subclass of tk.Frame and add to it
        tk.Frame.__init__(self, master, **style)

        # Divide into button area and toolbar name
        self.buttonframe = tk.Frame(self, **style)
        self.buttonframe.pack(side="top", fill="y", expand=True)
        self.name_label = tk.Label(self, **style_namelabel_normal)
        self.name_label["text"] = toolbarname
```

```
        self.name_label.pack(side="bottom")

    def add_button(self, icon=None, **kwargs):
        button = IconButton(self.buttonframe)
        options = {"text":"", "width":48, "height":32,
"compound":"top"}
        options.update(kwargs)
        if icon:
            button.set_icon(icon, **options)
        else:
            button.config(**options)
        button.pack(side="left", padx=2, pady=0, anchor="center")
        return button
```

The Ribbon tab system

Next up is the **Ribbon** widget, which, inspired by newer versions of Microsoft Office, will give our application not only a sleek modern look, but also the level of organization and simplicity that we need, to avoid scaring off the not-so-technical users of our application. Just like related buttons were grouped together into toolbars in the previous section, toolbars can here be grouped into the Ribbon tab areas at the top of the window that can be switched and flipped-between, like a notebook, as shown in the following screenshot:

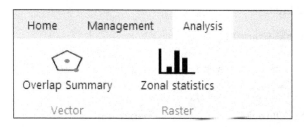

After creating the app/toolkit/ribbon.py module in the toolkit package, we begin with importing and styling, using a subtle grey highlight effect for the tab selectors:

```
# Import GUI
import Tkinter as tk

# Import internals
from .toolbars import *

# Import style
from . import theme
```

```
style_ribbon_normal = {"bg": theme.color3,
                       "height": 120,
                       "pady": 0}

style_tabsarea_normal = {"bg": theme.color3,
                         "height": 20,
                         "padx": 1,
                         "pady": 0}

style_tabselector_normal = {"bg": theme.color3,
                            "activebackground": theme.color4,
                            "fg": theme.font1["color"],
                            "font": theme.font1["type"],
                            "relief": "flat",
                            "padx":10, "pady":5}
style_tabselector_mouseover = {"bg": "Grey93" }

style_toolbarsarea_normal = {"bg": theme.color4}
```

The `Ribbon` class itself is a frame, with a top area for tab selectors, and the bottom area for displaying the currently selected tab area for related toolbars. Tabs are created as separate instances and added with the `add_tab` method, which will create a tab selector for that tab, which also lights up when the mouse hovers over it. A `switch` method will be called when a tab selector is pushed, which raises its tab area into view over all other tabs:

```
class Ribbon(tk.Frame):
    """
    Can switch between a series of logically grouped toolbar areas
    (tabs).
    """
    def __init__(self, master, **kwargs):
        # get theme style
        style = style_ribbon_normal.copy()
        style.update(kwargs)

        # Make this class a subclass of tk.Frame and add to it
        tk.Frame.__init__(self, master, **style)

        # Make top area for tab selectors
        self.tabs_area = tk.Frame(self, **style_tabsarea_normal)
        self.tabs_area.pack(fill="x", side="top")

        # Make bottom area for each tab's toolbars
```

```python
        self.toolbars_area = tk.Frame(self,
**style_toolbarsarea_normal)
        self.toolbars_area.pack(fill="both", expand=True,
side="top")
        self.pack_propagate(False)

        # Create tab list
        self.tabs = dict()

    def add_tab(self, tabname):
        tab = Tab(self.toolbars_area, tabname=tabname)
        self.tabs[tab.name] = tab
        self.current = tab
        # add tab to toolbars area
        tab.place(relwidth=1, relheight=1)
        # add tabname to tab selector area
        tab.selector = tk.Label(self.tabs_area, text=tab.name,
**style_tabselector_normal)
        tab.selector.pack(side="left", padx=5)
        # enable dynamic tab selector styling
        def mouse_in(event):
            if event.widget["state"] == "normal":
                event.widget.config(style_tabselector_mouseover)
        def mouse_out(event):
            if event.widget["state"] == "normal":
                event.widget.config(style_tabselector_normal)
        tab.selector.bind("<Enter>", mouse_in)
        tab.selector.bind("<Leave>", mouse_out)
        # make tab selector selectable
        tab.selector.bind("<Button-1>", self.switch)
        return tab

    def switch(self, event=None, tabname=None):
        if event: tabname = event.widget["text"]
        # deactivate old tab
        self.current.selector["state"] = "normal"
        # activate new tab
        self.current = self.tabs[tabname]
        self.current.selector.config(style_tabselector_normal)
        self.current.selector["state"] = "active"
        self.current.lift()
```

When we use the Ribbon's `add_tab` method it returns to us a `Tab` class, which it is up to us to populate with buttons and other content. For convenience, we give the `Tab` class an `add_toolbar` method:

```python
class Tab(tk.Frame):
    """
    Base class for all tabs
    """
    def __init__(self, master, tabname, **kwargs):
        # get theme style
        style = style_toolbarsarea_normal.copy()
        style.update(kwargs)

        # Make this class a subclass of tk.Frame and add to it
        tk.Frame.__init__(self, master, **style)

        # remember name
        self.name = tabname

    def add_toolbar(self, toolbarname):
        toolbar = Toolbar(self, toolbarname=toolbarname)
        toolbar.pack(side="left", padx=10, pady=0, fill="y")
        return toolbar
```

The bottom status bar

Another important GUI element is the status bar, which can contain one or more pieces of information or statuses and tends to be placed at the bottom of the application window meshed into the background. We create the `app/toolkit/statusbar.py` module and do the usual imports and styling in the beginning:

```python
# Import GUI
import Tkinter as tk

# Import style
from . import theme
style_statusbar_normal = {"height": 25,
                          "bg": theme.color3}
style_status_normal = {"fg": theme.font2["color"],
                       "font": theme.font2["type"],
                       "bg": theme.color3}
style_taskstatus_normal = style_status_normal.copy()
style_taskstatus_working = {"fg": theme.font1["color"],
                            "font": theme.font1["type"],
                            "bg": theme.strongcolor2}
```

The StatusBar widget itself is simply a frame that contains one or more status widgets. Here is the code for the StatusBar class:

```
class StatusBar(tk.Frame):
    def __init__(self, master, **kwargs):
        """
        A container bar that contains one or more status widgets
        """
        # get theme style
        style = style_statusbar_normal.copy()
        style.update(kwargs)

        # Make this class a subclass of tk.Frame and add to it
        tk.Frame.__init__(self, master, **style)

        # Insert status items
        self.task = TaskStatus(self)
        self.task.place(relx=0.0, rely=0.5, anchor="w")
        self.projection = ProjectionStatus(self)
        self.projection.place(relx=0.20, rely=0.5, anchor="w")
        self.zoom = ZoomStatus(self)
        self.zoom.place(relx=0.40, rely=0.5, anchor="w")
        self.mouse = MouseStatus(self)
        self.mouse.place(relx=0.70, rely=0.5, anchor="w")
```

We then make a base class for all status widgets called Status and some subclasses of it for displaying projection name, zoom level, and mouse pointer coordinates, without any event bindings or behavior since this will be controlled by a parent widget. A special TaskStatus widget can be set to start() and will turn orange along with a task description provided by the caller. It will return to normal once the stop method is called, as shown in the following code:

```
class Status(tk.Label):
    def __init__(self, master, **kwargs):
        """
        The base class used for all status widgets
        """
        # get theme style
        style = style_status_normal.copy()
        style.update(kwargs)

        # Make this class a subclass of tk.Label and add to it
        tk.Label.__init__(self, master, **style)
        self.prefix = ""
```

```
        def set_text(self, text):
            self["text"] = self.prefix + text

        def clear_text(self):
            self["text"] = self.prefix

class TaskStatus(Status):
    def __init__(self, master, **kwargs):
        # Make this class a subclass of tk.Label and add to it
        default = {"width":30, "anchor":"w"}
        default.update(kwargs)
        Status.__init__(self, master, **default)

        # Set startup status
        self.set_text("Ready")

    def start(self, taskname):
        self.config(**style_taskstatus_working)
        self.set_text(taskname)

    def stop(self):
        self.set_text("Finished!")
        self.config(**style_taskstatus_normal)
        def reset_text():
            self.set_text("Ready")
        self.after(1000, reset_text)

class ProjectionStatus(Status):
    def __init__(self, master, **kwargs):
        # Make this class a subclass of tk.Label and add to it
        self.prefix = "Map Projection: "
        default = {"text":self.prefix, "width":30, "anchor":"w"}
        default.update(kwargs)
        Status.__init__(self, master, **default)

class ZoomStatus(Status):
    def __init__(self, master, **kwargs):
        # Make this class a subclass of tk.Label and add to it
        self.prefix = "Horizontal Scale: "
        default = {"text":self.prefix, "width":30, "anchor":"w"}
        default.update(kwargs)
        Status.__init__(self, master, **default)
```

```
class MouseStatus(Status):
    def __init__(self, master, **kwargs):
        # Make this class a subclass of tk.Label and add to it
        self.prefix = "Mouse coordinates: "
        default = {"text":self.prefix, "width":50, "anchor":"w"}
        default.update(kwargs)
        Status.__init__(self, master, **default)
```

The layers pane

A crucial element in most GIS applications is the layers pane, which displays and allows access to the loaded data and shows their symbols and in which order they are rendered to the map. After initiating our new app/toolkit/layers.py module, we start it with some imports and styling. Note that we also import our top-level pythongis package and our dispatch module because this layer's pane needs to be able to load and render data:

```
# Import GUI functionality
import Tkinter as tk
from tkFileDialog import askopenfilenames, asksaveasfilename


# Import internals
from .buttons import *
from .popups import *


# Import style
from . import theme
style_layerspane_normal = {"bg": theme.color4,
                           "width": 200}
style_layersheader = {"bg": theme.color2,
                      "font": theme.titlefont1["type"],
                      "fg": theme.titlefont1["color"],
                      "anchor": "w", "padx": 5}

style_layeritem_normal = {"bg": theme.color4,
                          "width": 200,
                          "relief": "ridge"}
style_layercheck = {"bg": theme.color4}
style_layername_normal = {"bg": theme.color4,
                          "fg": theme.font1["color"],
                          "font": theme.font1["type"],
                          "relief": "flat",
                          "anchor": "w"}
```

```
# Import GIS functionality
import pythongis as pg
from . import dispatch
```

For now we only create the styled `LayersPane` class, with a title header text saying **Layers** and a main list area where individual loaded layers will show up. More about these layer items, how to load them, and their appearance and behavior will be dealt with more naturally in *Chapter 4, Rendering Our Geodata*:

```
class LayersPane(tk.Frame):
    def __init__(self, master, layer_rightclick=None, **kwargs):
        # get theme style
        style = style_layerspane_normal.copy()
        style.update(kwargs)

        # Make this class a subclass of tk.Frame and add to it
        tk.Frame.__init__(self, master, **style)

        # Make the top header
        self.header = tk.Label(self, text="Layers:",
**style_layersheader)
        self.header.pack(side="top", fill="x")

        # Then, the layer list view
        self.layersview = tk.Frame(self, **style)
        self.layersview.pack(side="top", fill="x")
        self.pack_propagate(False) # important, this prevents
layeritem names from deciding the size of layerspane
```

The Map widget

Last but not least, we cannot have a GIS without a Map widget for interactively viewing geographic data. Create the `app/toolkit/map.py` module and start it off as follows:

```
# Import builtins
import time

# Import GUI libraries
import Tkinter as tk

# Import internals
from .popups import popup_message
from .. import icons
```

```
# Import GIS functionality
import pythongis as pg
from . import dispatch

# Import style
from . import theme
style_map_normal = {"bg": theme.color1}
```

As with the layers pane, we begin developing the Map widget more fully in *Chapter 4, Rendering Our Geodata*, so for now we only make the initial `MapView` class. Eventually, we want our Map widget to be able to hold a rendered map image and let the user pan around and zoom in and out of it, so we make it a subclass of the Tkinter **Canvas** widget. Since the `MapView` class will be calling some potentially heavy rendering operations later on, we also need a way to link it to a status bar in order to report its progress:

```
class MapView(tk.Canvas):
    def __init__(self, master, **kwargs):
        # get theme style
        style = style_map_normal.copy()
        style.update(kwargs)

        # Make this class a subclass of tk.Canvas and add to it
        tk.Canvas.__init__(self, master, **style)

        # Other
        self.proj = kwargs.get("projection", "WGS84")
        self.statusbar = None
        self.mousepressed = False
        self.mouse_mode = "pan"
        self.zoomcenter = None
        self.zoomfactor = 1
        self.zoomdir = None
        self.last_zoomed = None

    def assign_statusbar(self, statusbar):
        statusbar.mapview = self
        self.statusbar = statusbar
```

Pop-up windows

Later in the book, there are several times we will need to open additional windows on top of our main GUI window, whether it be an error message or an options or tool menu. In our `toolkit` package, we therefore want to define some window templates.

 These window templates are not the same as the actual windows specific to our application, which are defined throughout the book as part of the `app/dialogues.py` module we created earlier in this chapter.

Create a module for window templating as `app/toolkit/popups.py` and begin with some imports:

```
# Import GUI helpers
import Tkinter as tk
import tkMessageBox

# Import internals
from .buttons import IconButton, OkButton, CancelButton
from . import dispatch
from ... import vector

# Define some styles
from . import theme
style_options_helptext = {"font": theme.font1["type"],
                          "fg": theme.font1["color"]}
style_options_titles = {"font": theme.titlefont1["type"],
                        "fg": theme.titlefont1["color"]}
style_options_labels = {"font": theme.font1["type"],
                        "fg": theme.font1["color"]}
```

First, we create some basic pop-up windows and templates. This includes a simple warning `popup_message` function that can be used to raise errors in the GUI, as well as a basic `Window` class template with ideal positioning and size, used as the starting point for any other window:

```
def popup_message(parentwidget, errmsg):
    tkMessageBox.showwarning("Warning", errmsg)

class Window(tk.Toplevel):
    def __init__(self, master=None, **kwargs):
        # Make this class a subclass of tk.Menu and add to it
        tk.Toplevel.__init__(self, master, **kwargs)
```

```
        # Set its size to percent of screen size, and place in
middle
        width = self.winfo_screenwidth() * 0.6
        height = self.winfo_screenheight() * 0.6
        xleft = self.winfo_screenwidth()/2.0 - width / 2.0
        ytop = self.winfo_screenheight()/2.0 - height / 2.0
        self.geometry("%ix%i+%i+%i"%(width, height, xleft, ytop))
        # Force and lock focus to the window
        self.grab_set()
        self.focus_force()
```

We also create another template, this time specifically for building tool options input frames. This will not be a window, but a Tkinter frame that can be placed inside any other widget, representing some tool or functionality where the user can customize settings or parameters and decide to run the tool or cancel. Let's create this generic RunToolFrame class, which consists of an input area where all the options will be built to the left, a help area on the right, and a button for running the tool on the bottom:

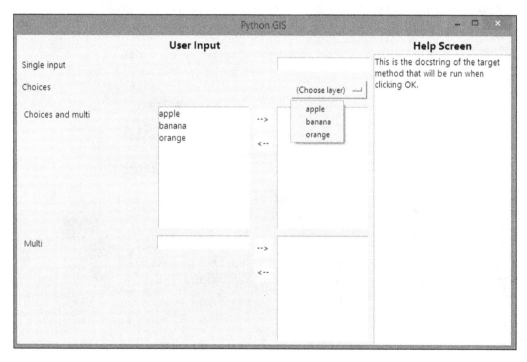

Here is the code to create the `RunToolFrame` class:

```
class RunToolFrame(tk.Frame):
    def __init__(self, master=None, **kwargs):
        # Make this class a subclass of tk.Toplevel and add to it
        tk.Frame.__init__(self, master, **kwargs)

        # Create empty option and input data
        self.hidden_options = dict()
        self.inputs = list()
        self.statusbar = None
        self.method = None
        self.process_results = None

        # Make helpscreen area to the right
        self.helpscreen = tk.Frame(self)
        self.helpscreen.pack(side="right", fill="y")
        self.helptitle = tk.Label(self.helpscreen, text="Help
Screen", **style_options_titles)
        self.helptitle.pack(fill="x")
        self.helptext = tk.Text(self.helpscreen, width=30,
                                wrap=tk.WORD, cursor="arrow",
                                **style_options_helptext)
        self.helptext.pack(fill="both", expand=True)

        # Make main screen where input goes to the left
        self.mainscreen = tk.Frame(self)
        self.mainscreen.pack(side="left", fill="both",
expand=True)
        self.maintitle = tk.Label(self.mainscreen, text="User
Input", **style_options_titles)
        self.maintitle.pack()
        self.mainoptions = tk.Frame(self.mainscreen)
        self.mainoptions.pack(fill="both", expand=True)
        self.mainbottom = tk.Frame(self.mainscreen)
        self.mainbottom.pack()

        # Make run button at bottom
        self.runbut = OkButton(self.mainbottom, command=self.run)
        self.runbut.pack(side="right")
```

To make things easier for us later, we also give it simple methods for defining which options to pass to the target operation, which it uses to automatically create the appropriate input widgets. The most powerful feature here is `add_option_input()` which adds a customizable option widget and has several arguments that can be tweaked and combined to produce widgets for many different value types. This requires two arguments: `label`—the text to display next to the input widget, and `valuetype`—a function to convert input values as retrieved from the widget (which is always text) into the type that the target operation expects.

If no other arguments are specified, this method adds an unnamed list argument to the target function, or by specifying `argname` you can make it a keyword argument. When the `multi` argument is true, the user is given an entry widget for freely typing in values and adding it to a list of option values, and if the `choices` argument is also true then the user is limited to choose one or more items from a list of choices. Setting the `choices` argument without the `multi` argument lets the user choose only a single value from a drop-down list of choices. The `default` argument defines the starting value of the widget, and `minval` and `maxval` tries to ensure that the final argument is greater than, less than, or between certain limits. Finally, there is also an `add_hidden_option` method that sets an option without having it show up as customizable widget. Take a look at the following code:

```
def add_option_input(self, label, valuetype, argname=None,
multi=False, length=None, default=None, minval=None,
maxval=None, choices=None):
        optionrow = tk.Frame(self.mainoptions)
        optionrow.pack(fill="x", anchor="n", pady=5, padx=5)
        if multi:
            # make a list-type widget that user can add to
            inputlabel = tk.Label(optionrow, text=label,
**style_options_labels)
            inputlabel.pack(side="left", anchor="nw", padx=3)
            inputwidget = tk.Listbox(optionrow,
activestyle="none",
                                    highlightthickness=0,
selectmode="extended",
                                    **style_options_labels)
            inputwidget.pack(side="right", anchor="ne", padx=3)

            if choices:
                # add a listbox of choices to choose from
                def addtolist():
                    for selectindex in fromlist.curselection():
                        selectvalue = fromlist.get(selectindex)
                        inputwidget.insert(tk.END, selectvalue)
```

```
                    for selectindex in
reversed(fromlist.curselection()):
                        fromlist.delete(selectindex)
                def dropfromlist():
                    for selectindex in inputwidget.curselection():
                        selectvalue = inputwidget.get(selectindex)
                        fromlist.insert(tk.END, selectvalue)
                    for selectindex in
reversed(inputwidget.curselection()):
                        inputwidget.delete(selectindex)
                # define buttons to send back and forth bw choices
and input
                buttonarea = tk.Frame(optionrow)
                buttonarea.pack(side="right", anchor="n")
                addbutton = IconButton(buttonarea,
command=addtolist,
                                        text="-->",
**style_options_labels)
                addbutton.pack(anchor="ne", padx=3, pady=3)
                dropbutton = IconButton(buttonarea,
command=dropfromlist,
                                        text="<--",
**style_options_labels)
                dropbutton.pack(anchor="ne", padx=3, pady=3)
                # create and populate the choices listbox
                fromlist = tk.Listbox(optionrow,
activestyle="none",
                                        highlightthickness=0,
selectmode="extended",
                                        **style_options_labels)
                for ch in choices:
                    fromlist.insert(tk.END, ch)
                fromlist.pack(side="right", anchor="ne", padx=3)
            else:
                # add a freeform entry field and button to add to
the listbox
                def addtolist():
                    entryvalue = addentry.get()
                    inputwidget.insert(tk.END, entryvalue)
                    addentry.delete(0, tk.END)
                def dropfromlist():
                    for selectindex in
reversed(inputwidget.curselection()):
                        inputwidget.delete(selectindex)
                buttonarea = tk.Frame(optionrow)
```

```
                    buttonarea.pack(side="right", anchor="n")
                    addbutton = IconButton(buttonarea, command=addtolist,
                                            text="-->",
**style_options_labels)
                    addbutton.pack(anchor="ne", padx=3, pady=3)
                    dropbutton = IconButton(buttonarea,
command=dropfromlist,
                                            text="<--",
**style_options_labels)
                    dropbutton.pack(anchor="ne", padx=3, pady=3)
                    # place the freeform text entry widget
                    addentry = tk.Entry(optionrow,
**style_options_labels)
                    addentry.pack(side="right", anchor="ne", padx=3)

        else:
            inputlabel = tk.Label(optionrow, text=label,
**style_options_labels)
            inputlabel.pack(side="left", anchor="nw")
            if choices:
                # dropdown menu of choices
                choice = tk.StringVar()
                if default: choice.set(default)
                inputwidget = tk.OptionMenu(optionrow, choice,
*choices)
                inputwidget.choice = choice
                inputwidget.pack(side="right", anchor="ne",
padx=3)
            else:
                # simple number or string entry widget
                inputwidget = tk.Entry(optionrow,
**style_options_labels)
                inputwidget.pack(side="right", anchor="ne")
                if default != None:
                    inputwidget.insert(tk.END, str(default))

        # remember for later
        inputwidget.meta = dict(argname=argname, label=label,
choices=choices,
                                valuetype=valuetype, multi=multi,
length=length,
                                default=default, minval=minval,
maxval=maxval)
        self.inputs.append(inputwidget)

    def add_hidden_option(self, argname, value):
        self.hidden_options[argname] = value
```

We now have ways to build a series of customizable parameter widgets in the window, but we still do not know what action or target operation should be run once the user is ready to run the tool window. This action must be given as a function able to receive the input widget parameters to `set_target_method()`. Doing so remembers the target function for later and retrieves the `doc` string from the given function and displays it to the user in the help area of the window. Also, we don't want to lock the GUI while the function is running, so the target function is dispatched in a new thread (more on this shortly). Using `assign_statusbar()` lets it inform a linked status bar while awaiting the results. We must also set a function to be run once processing the results is finished, using `set_finished_method()`:

```python
    def assign_statusbar(self, statusbar):
        self.statusbar = statusbar

    def set_target_method(self, taskname, method):
        self.taskname = taskname
        self.method = method
        # use the method docstring as the help text
        doc = method.__doc__
        if doc:
            # clean away tabs, multispaces, and other junk
            cleandoc =
  method.__doc__.strip().replace("\t","").replace("  "," ")
            # only keep where there are two newlines after each
other
            # because single newlines are likely just in-code
formatting
            cleandoc =
"\n\n".join(paragraph.replace("\n","").strip() for paragraph in
cleandoc.split("\n\n") )
            helptext = cleandoc
        else:
            helptext = "Sorry, no documentation available..."
        self.helptext.insert(tk.END, helptext)
        self.helptext["state"] = tk.DISABLED

    def set_finished_method(self, method):
        self.process_results = method

    def get_options(self):
        args = list()
        kwargs = dict()
        for key,val in self.hidden_options.items():
            if key == None: args.extend(val) #list arg
```

```
                else: kwargs[key] = val
        for inputwidget in self.inputs:
            argname = inputwidget.meta["argname"]
            multi = inputwidget.meta["multi"]
            choices = inputwidget.meta["choices"]
            valuetype = inputwidget.meta["valuetype"]

            # ensure within min/max range
            def validate(value):
                minval = inputwidget.meta["minval"]
                if minval and not value >= minval:
                    return Exception("The input value for %s was
smaller than the minimum value %s" %(inputwidget.meta["label"],
minval))
                maxval = inputwidget.meta["maxval"]
                if maxval and not value <= maxval:
                    return Exception("The input value for %s was
larger than the maximum value %s" %(inputwidget.meta["label"],
minval))
                return value

            # get value based on the argument type
            if argname == None:
                # if argname is None, then it is not a kwarg, but
unnamed arg list
                get = inputwidget.get(0, last=tk.END)
                if get != "":
                    args.extend( [validate(valuetype(val)) for val
in get] )
            elif multi:
                get = inputwidget.get(0, last=tk.END)
                if get != "":
                    kwargs[argname] = [ validate(valuetype(val))
for val in get ]
            elif choices:
                get = inputwidget.choice.get()
                if get != "":
                    kwargs[argname] = validate(valuetype(get))
            else:
                get = inputwidget.get()
                if get != "":
                    kwargs[argname] = validate(valuetype(get))
        return args,kwargs
```

```
def run(self):
    # first ensure the tool has been prepped correctly
    if not self.statusbar:
        raise Exception("Internal error: The tool has not been
assigned a statusbar")
    if not self.method:
        raise Exception("Internal error: The tool has not been
assigned a method to be run")
    if not self.process_results:
        raise Exception("Internal error: The tool has not been
assigned how to process the results")

    # get options
    try:
        args,kwargs = self.get_options()
    except Exception as err:
        popup_message(self, "Invalid options: \n" + str(err) )
        return

    # start statusbar
    self.statusbar.task.start(self.taskname)

    # run task
    pending = dispatch.request_results(self.method, args=args,
kwargs=kwargs)

    # schedule to process results upon completion
    def finish(results):
        # first run user specified processing
        try:
            self.process_results(results)
        except Exception as err:
            popup_message(self, "Error processing results:" +
"\n\n" + str(err) )
        # then stop the task
        self.statusbar.task.stop()
    # note: this window cannot be the one to schedule the
listening
    # ...because this window might be destroyed, so use its
master
    dispatch.after_completion(self.master, pending, finish)
```

Dispatching heavy tasks to thread workers

In later chapters, we will begin adding a specific GIS code to be run whenever we click on different buttons. Many GIS tasks can be quite heavy duty and take some time to finish. If we just run this lengthy code from within our Tkinter main event handling loop, then we will end up freezing our application while waiting for it to finish. To avoid such freezing, the long-running thread must be run in a thread other than our GUI, while our GUI checks at regular intervals to see if the results are in.

Since we expect to call on such heavy tasks quite frequently via button clicks, we simplify the threading procedure by creating an `app/toolkit/dispatch.py` module to do the work for us. Whenever a GUI tool or button needs to run any type of geospatial task or workload, we simply send the function and arguments over to the dispatch's `request_results` method. That method will immediately return a **Queue communications object**, which we must then send to `after_completion()` to check for the results at regular intervals without blocking any new GUI events or interaction, and run the specified function for processing the results once completed. If an exception is raised during the threaded processing, it will be returned to the application for proper handling.

Here is the code:

```python
import threading
import Queue
import traceback

def request_results(func, args=(), kwargs={}):
    # prepare request
    results = Queue.Queue()
    func_args = (args, kwargs)
    instruct = func, func_args, results

    # ask the thread
    worker = threading.Thread(target=_compute_results_,
args=instruct)
    worker.daemon = True
    worker.start()

    # return the empty results, it is up to the GUI to wait for it
    return results

def after_completion(window, queue, func):

    def check():
        try:
```

```
                result = queue.get(block=False)
            except:
                window.after(1000, check)
            else:
                func(result)

    window.after(100, check)

def _compute_results_(func, func_args, results):
    """
    This is where the actual work is done,
    and is run entirely in the new worker thread.
    """
    args, kwargs = func_args
    try: _results = func(*args, **kwargs)
    except Exception as errmsg:
        _results = Exception(traceback.format_exc() )
    results.put( _results )
```

Using the toolkit to build the GUI

Now that we have created the fundamental GUI building blocks, we just need to put them all together to create our first application:

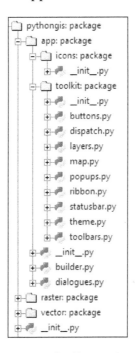

To do so, reopen the empty `app/builder.py` module we created at the beginning of this chapter. Let's create a basic GUI widget that represents the entirety of our application, populated with our widgets in a traditional layout:

- Our Ribbon widget at the top
- Our LayersPane on the left
- The MapView on the right
- The StatusBar container at the bottom

Here is the code:

```python
# Import builtins
import sys, os
import time

# Import GUI library
import Tkinter as tk

# Import internals
from .toolkit import *
from .dialogues import *

# Import GIS functionality
import pythongis as pg


class GUI(tk.Frame):
    def __init__(self, master, **kwargs):
        tk.Frame.__init__(self, master, **kwargs)

        # Place top ribbon area
        self.ribbon = Ribbon(self)
        self.ribbon.pack(side="top", fill="x")
        # Add tabs
        hometab = self.ribbon.add_tab("Home")
        # Set starting tab
        self.ribbon.switch(tabname="Home")

        # Place main middle area
        middle_area = tk.Frame(self)
        middle_area.pack(side="top", expand=True, fill="both")

        # Layers pane on left
```

```
self.layerspane = LayersPane(middle_area)
self.layerspane.pack(side="left", fill="y")

# Mapwidget on right
self.mapview = MapView(middle_area)
self.mapview.pack(side="left", fill="both", expand=True)

# Place bottom info and mouse coords bar at bottom
self.statusbar = StatusBar(self, height=20, width=100)
self.statusbar.pack(side="bottom", fill="x")

# Assign statusbar to widgets that perform actions
self.mapview.assign_statusbar(self.statusbar)
self.layerspane.assign_statusbar(self.statusbar)
```

Finally, we create a `run` function, which is separate from the GUI class, that simply creates the main Tkinter root window, packs our GUI widget inside it, and runs the application:

```
def run():
    """Build the GUI."""
    # create main window
    window = tk.Tk()
    window.wm_title("Python GIS")
    try: # windows and mac
        window.wm_state('zoomed')
    except: # linux
        window.wm_attributes("-zoomed", "1")
    # pack in the GUI frame
    gui = GUI(window)
    gui.place(relwidth=1, relheight=1)

    # open the window
    window.mainloop()
```

Make this function directly available from the `app` package, by adding the following to app/__init__.py:

```
from .builder import run
```

Testing our application

Provided you followed all of the instructions correctly, you should now be able to use the previous `run` function to begin exploring the application we have built so far. As we add more features throughout the book, you will likely want to call on this function repeatedly for testing purposes. Therefore, we add a ready-made script that does this for us called `guitester.py`, saving it in the same directory where our `pythongis` package is located to make the latter directly importable. The script only needs the following code:

```
import pythongis as pg
pg.app.run()
```

If you run `guitester.py` now, it should open an application that looks like this on Windows:

 You will also likely want to start collecting a few vector and raster files that you can use to test with the application later on. A good place to get them is http://www.naturalearthdata.com/, and they are all in the same WGS84 coordinate system.

Summary

At this point, we have made the basics of our application, one which doesn't do much right now but that is ready to be extended further as we continue to add new geospatial functionality. You learned to create a solid toolkit foundation of tools and widgets that we can use to build our GUI in a separate and flexible builder module, some of which will be extended in later chapters. The main missing piece, before we can say we have a functional GIS application, is to visualize data in our map widget. This is what we turn to in the next chapter.

4
Rendering Our Geodata

This chapter is likely to be one of the most interesting ones in this book. Geographic visualization of data is one of the core features of a GIS application, whether used as an exploratory aid or to produce a map. Learning geographic visualization should prove educational on different levels. In this chapter, you will learn how to do the following:

- Divide the rendering process into a series of renderings of one or more thematic layers
- Implement basic graphics renderings for vector and raster data, based on the view extent and zoom level
- Connect these renderings to our visual user interface, allowing interactive map visualization

Rendering

Typical usage in a GIS is to add one or more geographic data sources or layers to the application, which then gets immediately rendered in a map window. In *Chapter 3, Designing the Visual Look of Our Application,* we set this up as a MapView widget. Although the MapView widget is responsible to show the map in the interactive GUI, we want to separate the actual rendering logic in a module of its own. This way the user can also batch generate map renderings strictly through coding if they want.

Usually, graphics rendering is done most efficiently using the graphic capabilities of the user's hardware to draw on the screen. However, Tkinter's screen drawing capabilities (the Tkinter Canvas widget) can be slow, quickly runs out of memory if too many items are drawn, and produces only rough jagged graphics with no anti-aliased smoothing. We instead use the approach of drawing the graphics onto a virtual image, and then sending that image for display in Tkinter. This gives us a slight lag between rendering and display, and is not as fast as using graphics hardware; however, it is almost up there with the speed and quality of the existing GIS software and much better than the Tkinter default.

Installing PyAgg

Before we begin, we install the graphics rendering package that we will be using, called **PyAgg** created by the author. PyAgg is a high-level convenience wrapper around Fredrik Lundh's Python **aggdraw** bindings for the **Anti-Grain Geometry** C++ library. Compared to other popular rendering libraries like Matplotlib or Mapnik, PyAgg is incredibly lightweight at only about 2 MB and doesn't require advanced installation steps since it contains the necessary files precompiled. **PyCairo** is another lightweight graphics library, but while it has a much richer set of features, including line joins, line caps, and gradients, it turns out to be very slow at drawing large objects with many vertices. Therefore, we choose PyAgg for its lightness, its speed, and its convenient high level API.

Go ahead and install it now using the following steps:

1. In the Windows command line, write `C:/Python27/Scripts/pip install pyagg`

2. If for some reason that does not work, you can alternatively download the ZIP file from `https://github.com/karimbahgat/PyAgg` and extract it to the `site-packages` folder

3. Test that it imports correctly by typing `import pyagg` in Python shell

> If you want to go for other rendering libraries, Matplotlib has an easy-to-use Windows installer on their website. You should couple that with **Descartes** to convert geographic features to objects that Matplotlib can render, installed as pip install Descartes from the command line.
>
> For Mapnik, there are no precompiled version that I know of, so you will have to compile it on your own, following instructions from `http://wiki.openstreetmap.org/wiki/Mapnik/Installation`.
>
> If you want to try **PyCairo**, you can get a precompiled wheel file for Windows at `http://www.lfd.uci.edu/~gohlke/pythonlibs/#pycairo`.

Now that the necessary graphics library is installed, we make a module called `renderer.py` in the root of our `pythongis` folder. Initiate it with some imports:

```
import random
import pyagg
import PIL, PIL.Image
```

To make it accessible to our top-level `pythongis` package, just import it from inside `pythongis/__init__.py`:

```
from . import renderer
```

A sequence of layers

The basic idea of rendering in our GIS application is that we define a series of map layers that should be visualized together, such as countries, cities, and highways. For our convenience, we make this collection of layers into an iterable `LayerGroup` class with methods to add or remove layers, and a method for moving and changing the sequence in which these layers should be drawn. Note that it can hold references to one or more connected map widgets, letting it serve as a central layer repository for a split-view type of map application. Inside `renderer.py`, write the following code:

```python
class LayerGroup:
    def __init__(self):
        self.layers = list()
        self.connected_maps = list()

    def __iter__(self):
        for layer in self.layers:
            yield layer

    def add_layer(self, layer):
        self.layers.append(layer)

    def move_layer(self, from_pos, to_pos):
        layer = self.layers.pop(from_pos)
        self.layers.insert(to_pos, layer)

    def remove_layer(self, position):
        self.layers.pop(position)

    def get_position(self, layer):
        return self.layers.index(layer)
```

The MapCanvas drawer

Next, we need a way to combine the group of map layers into a final composite map image. For this we create a MapCanvas class, which is a wrapper around PyAgg's Canvas class. The MapCanvas class creates the final rendering by asking each layer to render themselves onto an image (with a transparent background), and then overlaying them on top of each other in the correct sequence. Since each layer has a separate image rendering, it is possible to reorder or remove layers very fast without having to redraw all the layers.

Layering images on top of each other is one thing, but how do we know which parts of our layers to show, or where on the drawing canvas they go? To do this, we need to transform the coordinates of our geospatial data to the pixel coordinates of our image, which is actually not any different from plotting arbitrary data values on a graph. Usually in 2D computer graphics, transforming from one coordinate system to another is done by multiplying each x and y coordinate with some precomputed numbers, called the **affine transform coefficients**. However, arriving at these coefficients is not immediately intuitive and requires a bit of matrix math.

PyAgg makes our lives easier, and this is one of the main reasons we chose to use it. With the custom_space method, PyAgg allows us to tell the Canvas instance to imagine that the image on which it draws is a representation of a given rectangular real-world space. This space is defined by a bounding box of coordinates so that all the incoming data for rendering is placed in relation to that coordinate system, drawing only those parts that fall within its boundaries. PyAgg then uses that bounding box to compute the transform coefficients behind the scenes, with the help of Sean Gillies' affine module. As another useful feature for us, PyAgg allows locking the aspect ratio of the requested view extents to have the same width and height ratio as the canvas image itself, to avoid the geographic data becoming distorted or stretched. Refer to the following figure:

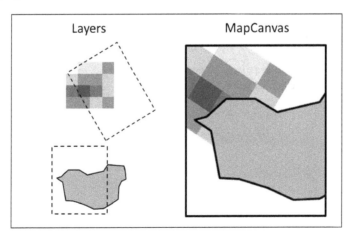

On startup, before having added any data, we set the default coordinate space of `MapCanvas` class with `geographic_space()`, which is just a wrapper around `custom_space()` using `[-180, 90, 180, -90]` as the bounds (the standard latitude longitude coordinate system of unprojected data) and enforces aspect ratio. By simply changing the coordinate space bounds, the `MapCanvas` class can be used to render absolutely any geographic data regardless of its coordinate system or CRS. This way, we can create the effect of zooming or panning the map by modifying the drawing transform coefficients. For this, we make use of PyAgg's convenient zooming methods that let us specify in human terms how we would like to zoom or pan the drawing transform.

One challenge, however, is when rendering data layers defined in different coordinate reference systems (CRS), as these will not line up as expected. The usual solution in GIS is to provide on-the-fly reprojection of all geographic data into a single common CRS. However, converting between geographic CRS involves a wide range of parameters and assumptions about the shape of the earth and the type of projection, which makes it more complicated than our previous affine transform. For these reasons and others, our application will not be dealing with CRS reprojection. So the main limitation of our `MapCanvas` class is that it needs all data to be in the same CRS in order to properly overlay them. We return briefly to the topic of CRS in *Chapter 8, Looking Forward*, and potential ways to add such functionality yourself. Here is the code for the `MapCanvas` class:

```
class MapCanvas:
    def __init__(self, layers, width, height, background=None,
*args, **kwargs):

        # remember and be remembered by the layergroup
        self.layers = layers
        layers.connected_maps.append(self)

        # create the drawer with a default unprojected lat-long
coordinate system
        self.drawer = pyagg.Canvas(width, height, background)
        self.drawer.geographic_space()

        self.img = self.drawer.get_image()

    def pixel2coord(self, x, y):
        return self.drawer.pixel2coord(x, y)

    # Map canvas alterations

    def offset(self, xmove, ymove):
        self.drawer.move(xmove, ymove)
```

```python
    def resize(self, width, height):
        self.drawer.resize(width, height, lock_ratio=True)
        self.img = self.drawer.get_image()

    # Zooming

    def zoom_bbox(self, xmin, ymin, xmax, ymax):
        self.drawer.zoom_bbox(xmin, ymin, xmax, ymax)

    def zoom_factor(self, factor, center=None):
        self.drawer.zoom_factor(factor, center=center)

    def zoom_units(self, units, center=None):
        self.drawer.zoom_units(units, center=center)

    # Drawing

    def render_one(self, layer):
        if layer.visible:
            layer.render(width=self.drawer.width,
                         height=self.drawer.height,
                    coordspace_bbox=self.drawer.coordspace_bbox)
            self.update_draworder()

    def render_all(self):
        for layer in self.layers:
            if layer.visible:
                layer.render(width=self.drawer.width,
                             height=self.drawer.height,
                             coordspace_bbox=self.drawer.coordspace_
bbox)
        self.update_draworder()

    def update_draworder(self):
        self.drawer.clear()
        for layer in self.layers:
            if layer.visible:
                self.drawer.paste(layer.img)
        self.img = self.drawer.get_image()

    def get_tkimage(self):
        # Special image format needed by Tkinter to display it in
    the GUI
        return self.drawer.get_tkimage()
```

Individual layer renderings

The `MapCanvas` class described previously was responsible to define a common coordinate space and combining the images of its layers, but not for any actual drawing. We leave this task to the individual layer classes, one for `vector` and one for `raster`.

Vector layers

The rendering of vector data is fairly easy. All we have to do is create a `VectorLayer` instance around the `VectorData` class, and optionally decide some style aspects of its geometries using keyword arguments. During this style options stage, we allow all features being styled in the same way.

 On your own, you may want to expand this with the ability to style individual features or groups of features based on their attribute values. This will allow you to visualize how data flows across space.

To render itself, the vector layer creates a PyAgg Canvas with the same image size as its parent `MapCanvas` class, on top of a transparent background. To make sure it only draws the parts of the data that its parent `MapCanvas` class is supposed to be seeing, it is up to us to set the `coordspace_bbox` argument with the bounding box of the `MapCanvas` class. The layer passes this information on to its `Canvas` instance via `custom_space()`, so that PyAgg can calculate the correct drawing transform coefficients using matrix math.

When it comes to drawing each feature, PyAgg and its underlying aggdraw module has different drawing methods with different requirements for how its coordinates should be formatted. Since our geometries can be either points, lines, or polygons and are stored in GeoJSON formatted dictionaries, we need to translate our GeoJSON format to that which is expected by PyAgg. For instance, a GeoJSON polygon is a list of coordinate sequences, the first one being the exterior and all subsequent ones its holes; this information can then be sent to the PyAgg's `draw_polygon` method with the arguments it expects. Instead of us learning the entire GeoJSON format to correctly parse the data and call on the right methods, PyAgg's `Canvas` class can do this for us in the `draw_geojson` method. After drawing, the rendered image is remembered and made accessible to `MapCanvas`:

```
class VectorLayer:
    def __init__(self, data, **options):

        self.data = data
        self.visible = True
```

```
        self.img = None

        # by default, set random style color
        rand = random.randrange
        randomcolor = (rand(255), rand(255), rand(255), 255)
        self.styleoptions = {"fillcolor": randomcolor}

        # override default if any manually specified styleoptions
        self.styleoptions.update(options)

    def render(self, width, height, coordspace_bbox):
        drawer = pyagg.Canvas(width, height, background=None)
        drawer.custom_space(*coordspace_bbox)
        # get features based on spatial index, for better speeds
when zooming
        if not hasattr(self.data, "spindex"):
            self.data.create_spatial_index()
        spindex_features = self.data.quick_overlap(coordspace_bbox)
        # draw each as geojson, using same style options for all
features
        for feat in spindex_features:
            drawer.draw_geojson(feat.geometry,
**self.styleoptions)
        self.img = drawer.get_image()
```

Raster layers

In a similar manner, rendering raster data is done by creating a `RasterLayer` class. When rendering itself, consider that each cell in a raster grid has a precise location and rectangular area that it covers in geographic space. To transform these cell coordinates from raster space to image space for visualization, the `RasterLayer` class has to know the coordinate view extent of the parent `MapCanvas` class and find where and how each raster cell should be placed within those bounds.

Luckily for us, we already gave the `RasterData` class a method for doing this type of grid transform, namely, the `positioned` method that leverages PIL's quad transform technique. Using this method, the `RasterLayer` class specifies the width and height of the data it wants to return, based on the size of its parent `MapCanvas` class, and to only include the parts of the raster that are within the bounds of the `MapCavas` classes' coordinate system.

Since the data structure of our RasterData class is based on PIL images, all it has to do is combine all band images together to create a gray scale or RGB image, ready to be added to the MapCanvas class for visualization. The positioned method also transforms and returns the nodata mask that the RasterLayer class uses to make missing values transparent.

 Currently, we do not allow customization of the colors used for visualizing the raster, but that should be an easy feature to add if you want to, using the PIL's support for color palettes.

```python
class RasterLayer:
    def __init__(self, data, **options):
        self.data = data
        self.styleoptions = dict(**options)
        self.visible = True
        self.img = None

    def render(self, width, height, coordspace_bbox):
        # position in space
        positioned,mask = self.data.positioned(width, height,
coordspace_bbox)

        # combine all data bands into one image for visualizing
        if len(positioned.bands) == 1:
            # greyscale if one band
            band1 = positioned.bands[0]
            img = band1.img.convert("RGB")
        else:
            # rgb of first three bands
            bands = [band.img for band in positioned.bands[:3] ]
            img = PIL.Image.merge("RGB", bands)

        # make edge and nodata mask transparent
        img.putalpha(mask)

        # final
        self.img = img
```

Interactively rendering our maps

Now that we have ways of combining several layers into a rendered map image, we get to the more exciting part of how to do this interactively in our application with immediate results.

Linking the MapView to the renderer

After we rendered a set of layers onto a map image, this image must be sent to and displayed in our application for immediate feedback. This task is done by the MapView widget we created in *Chapter 3, Designing the Visual Look of Our Application*. While building our application, the idea is that all we have to worry about is creating this visual MapView widget; behind the scenes, the MapView will be responsible for creating its own `MapCanvas` renderer to do the actual work. Since the `MapCanvas` class needs LayerGroup to manage its layers, we will create a MapView method to assign a LayerGroup, in `app/toolkit/map.py`:

```
def assign_layergroup(self, layergroup):
    self.layers = layergroup
```

We then link the two together as additional code in the MapView's __init__ method. Since the renderer requires a width and a height in pixels before it can be created, we schedule MapView to create it shortly after startup (because Tkinter won't know how much space is required for the various widgets before startup):

```
    # Assign a renderer just after startup, because only then
can one know the required window size
    def on_startup():
        # create renderer
        width, height = self.winfo_width(),
self.winfo_height()
        self.renderer = pg.MapCanvas(self.layers, width,
height)
        # link to self
        self.renderer.mapview = self
        # fill with blank image
        self.tkimg = self.renderer.get_tkimage()
        self.image_on_canvas = self.create_image(0, 0,
anchor="nw", image=self.tkimg )

    self.after(10, on_startup)
```

Requesting to render a map

Whenever the MapView widget wants to render a whole new map with all visible layers, it calls on this method, and does so in a separate thread in order to not freeze up the application while waiting for the results. It also updates the status bar on its activities and sets the horizontal scale status based on the new zoom level. Afterwards, it has to update the image that is placed on the viewable Tkinter Canvas:

```python
    def threaded_rendering(self):
        # perform render/zoom in separate thread
        self.statusbar.task.start("Rendering layers...")
        pending =
dispatch.request_results(self.renderer.render_all)

        def finish(result):
            if isinstance(result, Exception):
                popup_message(self, "Rendering error: " +
str(result) )
            else:
                # update renderings
                self.coords(self.image_on_canvas, 0, 0) # always
reanchor rendered image nw at 0,0 in case of panning
                self.update_image()
                # display zoom scale

    self.statusbar.zoom.set_text("1:"+str(self.renderer.drawer.
coordspace_units) )
                self.statusbar.task.stop()

        dispatch.after_completion(self, pending, finish)

    def update_image(self):
        self.tkimg = self.renderer.get_tkimage()
        self.itemconfig(self.image_on_canvas, image=self.tkimg )
```

Resizing the map in proportion to window resizing

If the user changes the application window size from the original startup size, we need to resize the MapView's renderer accordingly. We tell it to resize only after one-third of a second after the user has stopped resizing the window, because Tkinter's resize event is triggered continuously during the process. What is important in the event of such a resize is that the coordinate system is changed accordingly to map the new image dimensions; fortunately for us, our PyAgg Canvas automatically updates and locks the aspect ratio on the drawing transform for us when resizing:

```
# Schedule resize map on window resize
self.last_resized = None
def resizing(event):
    # record resize time
    self.last_resized = time.time()
    # schedule to check if finished resizing after x
millisecs
    self.after(300, process_if_finished)

def process_if_finished():
    # only if x time since last resize event
    if time.time() - self.last_resized > 0.3:
        width, height = self.winfo_width(),
self.winfo_height()
        self.renderer.resize(width, height)
        self.threaded_rendering()

self.bind("<Configure>", resizing)
```

The LayersPane as a LayerGroup

With a basic Map widget capable of rendering, we move onto adding data to the map, which we then can view in our application's layers pane. The LayersPane widget is merely a visual representation of the sequence of layers in its connected LayerGroup class. Therefore, the LayersPane class in the `app/toolkit/layers.py` file needs a method to bind it to a LayerGroup:

```
def assign_layergroup(self, layergroup):
    self.layers = layergroup
```

Adding layers

We will now create an `add_layer` method to the LayersPane class in `app/toolkit/layers.py`. To make it flexible, we allow it to add a layer either from a file path or from an already loaded data object.

If it detects a file path, it first runs a `from_filepath` function, where it decides whether to create a vector or raster data class, tells our dispatch module to use this data class to load the file path in a background thread, and schedules our application to check the results queue every 100 ms to see whether the loading is done.

Once loaded or if given an already loaded data object, it goes straight to adding the layer with the `from_loaded()` function. This creates a VectorLayer or RasterLayer capable of rendering itself, adds a representation of that layer responsive to right-click events in the LayersPane (more on this in the next section), and asks the dispatch to render the layer as an image and update the MapView widget(s) to which it is connected. If the new layer is the only one currently loaded in the LayersPanel, then we automatically zoom to its bounding box so that the user gets an immediate look at the data.

Here is the code:

```python
def add_layer(self, filepath_or_loaded, name=None, **kwargs):

    def from_filepath(filepath):
        if
filepath.lower().endswith((".shp",".geojson",".json")):
            func = pg.vector.data.VectorData
            args = (filepath,)
        elif filepath.lower().endswith((".asc",".ascii",
                                        ".tif",".tiff",".geotiff",
                                        ".jpg",".jpeg",
                                        ".png",".bmp",".gif")):
            func = pg.raster.data.RasterData
            args = (filepath,)
        else:
            popup_message(self, "Fileformat not supported\n\n"
+ filepath )
            return

        self.statusbar.task.start("Loading layer from
file...")

        pending = dispatch.request_results(func, args, kwargs)

        def finish(loaded):
```

```
            if isinstance(loaded, Exception):
                popup_message(self, str(loaded) + "\n\n" +
filepath )
            else:
                from_loaded(loaded)
            self.statusbar.task.stop()

        dispatch.after_completion(self, pending, finish)

    def from_loaded(loaded):
        # add the data as a rendering layer
        if isinstance(loaded, pg.vector.data.VectorData):
            renderlayer = pg.renderer.VectorLayer(loaded)
        elif isinstance(loaded, pg.raster.data.RasterData):
            renderlayer = pg.renderer.RasterLayer(loaded)
        self.layers.add_layer(renderlayer)

        # list a visual representation in the layerspane list
        listlayer = LayerItem(self.layersview,
renderlayer=renderlayer, name=name)
        listlayer.namelabel.bind("<Button-3>",
self.layer_rightclick)
        listlayer.pack(fill="x", side="bottom")

        # render to and update all mapcanvases connected to
the layergroup
        for mapcanvas in self.layers.connected_maps:
            if len(mapcanvas.layers.layers) == 1:
                # auto zoom to layer if it is the only layer
                mapcanvas.zoom_bbox(*loaded.bbox)

            func = mapcanvas.render_one
            args = [renderlayer]

            self.statusbar.task.start("Rendering layer...")
            pending = dispatch.request_results(func, args)

            def finish(loaded):
                if isinstance(loaded, Exception):
                    popup_message(self, "Rendering error: " +
str(loaded) )
                else:
                    mapcanvas.mapview.update_image()
                self.statusbar.task.stop()
```

```
                dispatch.after_completion(self, pending, finish)

        # load from file or go straight to listing/rendering
        if isinstance(filepath_or_loaded, (str,unicode)):
            from_filepath(filepath_or_loaded)
        else:
            from_loaded(filepath_or_loaded)
```

Editing layers in the LayersPane widget

Now that we can add layers to the LayersPane, we also want to be able to play around with the layers. A layer is represented as a LayerItem widget, which we have yet to define. We give the LayerItem a delete button on the right side, and a checkbox on the left side to toggle its visibility as shown in the following diagram:

The delete button is going to need an icon so let's start by getting one of those:

1. Go to an icon website such as www.iconarchive.com or http://www.flaticon.com.

2. Search for and choose an icon that you like.

3. Save it as delete_layer.png with 32 pixel size and place it in your app/icons folder.

We also define how to rename a layer's name, which temporarily adds a Tkinter entry widget over the layer's name display so the user can alter the name and press *Return* to accept or *ESC* to cancel. Now make the LayerItem class in app/toolkit/layers.py using the following code:

```
class LayerItem(tk.Frame):
    def __init__(self, master, renderlayer, name=None, **kwargs):
        # get theme style
        style = style_layeritem_normal.copy()
        style.update(kwargs)

        # Make this class a subclass of tk.Frame and add to it
        tk.Frame.__init__(self, master, **style)
        self.layerspane = self.master.master
        self.statusbar = self.layerspane.statusbar
```

```
        # Create a frame to place main row with name etc
        self.firstrow = tk.Frame(self, **style)
        self.firstrow.pack(side="top", fill="x", expand=True)

        # Create the visibility check box
        var = tk.BooleanVar(self)
        self.checkbutton = tk.Checkbutton(self.firstrow,
variable=var, offvalue=False, onvalue=True,
command=self.toggle_visibility, **style_layercheck)
        self.checkbutton.var = var
        self.checkbutton.pack(side="left")
        self.checkbutton.select()

        # Create Delete button to the right
        self.deletebutton = IconButton(self.firstrow, padx=2,
relief="flat", command=self.delete)
        self.deletebutton.set_icon("delete_layer.png")
        self.deletebutton.pack(side="right")

        # Create the layername display
        self.renderlayer = renderlayer
        if name: layername = name
        elif self.renderlayer.data.filepath:
            layername =
os.path.split(self.renderlayer.data.filepath)[-1]
        else: layername = "Unnamed layer"
        self.namelabel = tk.Label(self.firstrow, text=layername,
**style_layername_normal)
        self.namelabel.pack(side="left", fill="x", expand=True)

    def toggle_visibility(self):
        self.layerspane.toggle_layer(self)

    def delete(self):
        self.layerspane.remove_layer(self)

    def ask_rename(self):
        # place entry widget on top of namelabel
        nameentry = tk.Entry(self)
        nameentry.place(x=self.namelabel.winfo_x(),
y=self.namelabel.winfo_y(), width=self.namelabel.winfo_width(),
height=self.namelabel.winfo_height())
        # set its text to layername and select all text
```

```
nameentry.insert(0, self.namelabel["text"])
nameentry.focus()
nameentry.selection_range(0, tk.END)
# accept or cancel change via keypress events
def finish(event):
    newname = nameentry.get()
    nameentry.destroy()
    self.namelabel["text"] = newname
def cancel(event):
    nameentry.destroy()
nameentry.bind("<Return>", finish)
nameentry.bind("<Escape>", cancel)
```

The `LayerItem` class's delete button and visibility checkbox in the previous code both called on methods in the parent LayersPane to do the work, because the LayersPane's connected MapCanvas need updating afterwards. Therefore, let's add these methods to the LayersPane. We also need a way to specify the function to be run when right-clicking any of the layers in the LayersPane:

```
def toggle_layer(self, layeritem):
    # toggle visibility
    if layeritem.renderlayer.visible == True:
        layeritem.renderlayer.visible = False
    elif layeritem.renderlayer.visible == False:
        layeritem.renderlayer.visible = True
    # update all mapcanvas
    for mapcanvas in self.layers.connected_maps:
        mapcanvas.update_draworder()
        mapcanvas.mapview.update_image()

def remove_layer(self, layeritem):
    # remove from rendering
    layerpos = self.layers.get_position(layeritem.renderlayer)
    self.layers.remove_layer(layerpos)
    for mapcanvas in self.layers.connected_maps:
        mapcanvas.update_draworder()
        mapcanvas.mapview.update_image()
    # remove from layers list
    layeritem.destroy()

def bind_layer_rightclick(self, func):
    self.layer_rightclick = func
```

Click-and-drag to rearrange the layer sequence

A slightly more complicated procedure is to let the user rearrange the drawing order of the LayerItems in the LayersPane by clicking and dragging them to a new position. It is an essential feature of the layered nature of any GIS software, but unfortunately the Tkinter GUI framework does not provide us with any drag-and-drop shortcuts, so we must build it from scratch. We keep it simple and only allow one layer to be moved at a time.

To rearrange a layer in the list, we first need to listen for an event where the user clicks a LayerItem. In such an event, we remember the position of the layer that we want to move and change the cursor to indicate that a drag and drop is underway. When the user releases the mouse-click, we loop through the screen coordinates of all the LayerItem widgets to detect the layer position at which the mouse was released. Note that the index position of the layer that is rendered on top of all others is the first one in the list of LayerItems, but is the last one in the sequence of layers in the LayerGroup. We add this listening behavior in the LayerItem's __init__ method:

```
def start_drag(event):
    self.dragging = event.widget.master.master
    self.config(cursor="exchange")

def stop_drag(event):

    # find closest layerindex to release event
    def getindex(layeritem):
        return self.layerspane.layers.get_position(layeritem.
renderlayer)

    goingdown = event.y_root -
(self.dragging.winfo_rooty() + self.dragging.winfo_height() /
2.0) > 0
    if goingdown:
        i =
len(self.layerspane.layersview.winfo_children())
        for layeritem in
sorted(self.layerspane.layersview.winfo_children(),
key=getindex, reverse=True):
            if event.y_root < layeritem.winfo_rooty() +
layeritem.winfo_height() / 2.0:
                break
            i -= 1
    else:
        i = 0
```

```
                    for layeritem in
sorted(self.layerspane.layersview.winfo_children(),
key=getindex):
                            if event.y_root > layeritem.winfo_rooty() -
layeritem.winfo_height() / 2.0:
                            break
                    i += 1

            # move layer
            frompos =
self.layerspane.layers.get_position(self.dragging.renderlayer)
            if i != frompos:
                self.layerspane.move_layer(frompos, i)

            # clean up
            self.dragging = None
            self.config(cursor="arrow")

        self.dragging = None
        self.namelabel.bind("<Button-1>", start_drag)
        self.namelabel.bind("<ButtonRelease-1>", stop_drag)
```

After the user has interacted with the LayersPane to tell it where to move a layer, we tell its associated LayerGroup to rearrange the layer sequence based on the "from and to" positions. We then tell all of the MapCanvas connected to that LayerGroup to update their drawing order and the image being displayed. We must define this method in the LayersPane class:

```
def move_layer(self, fromindex, toindex):
    self.layers.move_layer(fromindex, toindex)
    for mapcanvas in self.layers.connected_maps:
        mapcanvas.update_draworder()
        mapcanvas.mapview.update_image()
    self.update_layerlist()
```

Zooming the map image

At this point, we can add and remove layers to and from the map and rearrange their sequence, but we still cannot interact with the map itself. Here comes one of the great things of making our own application. One thing that users may find difficult with existing GIS software is that they have to choose between one of two modes of interacting with the map: one is the **pan** mode so that clicking and dragging the mouse moves the map accordingly, and the other is the **rectangle-zoom** mode where click and drag defines the area to zoom to.

Switching between these two modes is not very conducive to map exploration which is often more of a dynamic and iterative process, involving simultaneous use of zooming and panning when using Google Maps. Now that we have the power to decide, let's combine zoom and pan by controlling them with double clicks and click and drag, respectively.

The actual zooming of the map is done by asking the MapCanvas to redraw the map at the given zoom level. We bind a 2x zoom factor method centered on the mouse to events where the user double clicks on the map. We give such zooming a one-third of a second lag after the user stops clicking so that the user can double click many times in a row for extra large zoom without overwhelming the application to render multiple incremental zoom images. Each time a zoom level is changed, we also ask to update the status bar's zoom unit scale, which is given to us by the PyAgg rendering canvas. All of this listening behavior we add to the MapView's __init__ method, inside app/toolkit/map.py:

```
        # Bind interactive zoom events
        def doubleleft(event):
            self.zoomfactor += 1
            canvasx,canvasy =
self.canvasx(event.x),self.canvasy(event.y)
            self.zoomcenter = self.renderer.pixel2coord(canvasx,
canvasy)
            self.zoomdir = "in"
            # record zoom time
            self.last_zoomed = time.time()
            # schedule to check if finished zooming after x
millisecs
            self.after(300, zoom_if_finished)

        def doubleright(event):
            self.zoomfactor += 1
            canvasx,canvasy =
self.canvasx(event.x),self.canvasy(event.y)
            self.zoomcenter = self.renderer.pixel2coord(canvasx,
canvasy)
            self.zoomdir = "out"
            # record zoom time
            self.last_zoomed = time.time()
            # schedule to check if finished zooming after x
millisecs
            self.after(300, zoom_if_finished)

        def zoom_if_finished():
            if time.time() - self.last_zoomed >= 0.3:
```

```
            if self.zoomdir == "out":
                self.zoomfactor *= -1
            self.renderer.zoom_factor(self.zoomfactor,
    center=self.zoomcenter)
            self.threaded_rendering()
            # reset zoomfactor
            self.zoomfactor = 1
            self.last_zoomed = None


        self.bind("<Double-Button-1>", doubleleft)
        self.bind("<Double-Button-3>", doubleright)
```

Map panning and one-time rectangle zoom

Panning the map is relatively easy since the rendered map image is simply an image placed inside a Tkinter scrollable Canvas widget. The rendered map image is always placed at the Tkinter Canvas' [0,0] coordinates in the top-left corner, but when we pan the map, we make the image start following the mouse. After we let go, the renderer begins rendering a new map by offsetting the MapCanvas' PyAgg coordinate system and rerendering the map. We also allow for an alternative zoom mode that uses these click and release events to perform a conventional rectangle zoom, along with the visual guide of Tkinter's built-in canvas rectangle drawing. This rectangle zoom mode should only be as a one-time event that defaults back to panning, since rectangle zoom is relatively rarely needed. To indicate when we are in rectangle zoom mode, we also replace the cursor with something like a magnifying glass icon whenever it is over the MapView widget, so you will need to find and save a `rect_zoom.png` image to `app/icons`. Moving the mouse over the map generally should also display the mouse coordinates in the status bar. We define this in the `__init__` method of the MapView widget, in `app/toolkit/map.py`:

```
        def mousepressed(event):
            if self.last_zoomed: return
            self.mousepressed = True
            self.startxy = self.canvasx(event.x),
    self.canvasy(event.y)
            if self.mouse_mode == "zoom":
                startx,starty = self.startxy
                self.rect = self.create_rectangle(startx, starty,
    startx+1, starty+1, fill=None)

        def mousemoving(event):
            if self.statusbar:
                # mouse coords
```

```
                    mouse = self.canvasx(event.x),
self.canvasy(event.y)
                    xcoord,ycoord = self.renderer.pixel2coord(*mouse)
                    self.statusbar.mouse.set_text("%3.8f , %3.8f"
%(xcoord,ycoord) )
            if self.mouse_mode == "pan":
                if self.mousepressed:
                    startx,starty = self.startxy
                    curx,cury = self.canvasx(event.x),
self.canvasy(event.y)
                    xmoved = curx - startx
                    ymoved = cury - starty
                    self.coords(self.image_on_canvas, xmoved,
ymoved) # offset the image rendering
            elif self.mouse_mode == "zoom":
                curx,cury = self.canvasx(event.x),
self.canvasy(event.y)
                    self.coords(self.zoomicon_on_canvas, curx, cury)
                if self.mousepressed:
                    startx,starty = self.startxy
                    self.coords(self.rect, startx, starty, curx,
cury)

        def mousereleased(event):
            if self.last_zoomed: return
            self.mousepressed = False
            if self.mouse_mode == "pan":
                startx,starty = self.startxy
                curx,cury = self.canvasx(event.x),
self.canvasy(event.y)
                xmoved = int(curx - startx)
                ymoved = int(cury - starty)
                if xmoved or ymoved:
                    # offset image rendering
                    self.renderer.offset(xmoved, ymoved)
                    self.threaded_rendering()
            elif self.mouse_mode == "zoom":
                startx,starty = self.startxy
                curx,cury = self.canvasx(event.x),
self.canvasy(event.y)
                    self.coords(self.rect, startx, starty, curx, cury)
                    # disactivate rectangle selector
                    self.delete(self.rect)
```

```
                self.event_generate("<Leave>") # fake a mouseleave
event to destroy icon
                self.mouse_mode = "pan"
                # make the zoom
                startx,starty =
self.renderer.drawer.pixel2coord(startx,starty)
                curx,cury =
self.renderer.drawer.pixel2coord(curx,cury)
                bbox = [startx, starty, curx, cury]
                self.renderer.zoom_bbox(*bbox)
                self.threaded_rendering()

        def mouseenter(event):
            if self.mouse_mode == "zoom":
                # replace mouse with zoomicon
                self.zoomicon_tk = icons.get("zoom_rect.png",
width=30, height=30)
                self.zoomicon_on_canvas =
self.create_image(event.x, event.y, anchor="center",
image=self.zoomicon_tk )
                self.config(cursor="none")

        def mouseleave(event):
            if self.mouse_mode == "zoom":
                # back to normal mouse
                self.delete(self.zoomicon_on_canvas)
                self.config(cursor="arrow")

        def cancel(event):
            if self.mouse_mode == "zoom":
                self.event_generate("<Leave>") # fake a mouseleave
event to destroy icon
                self.mouse_mode = "pan"
                if self.mousepressed:
                    self.delete(self.rect)

        # bind them
        self.bind("<Button-1>", mousepressed, "+")
        self.bind("<Motion>", mousemoving)
        self.bind("<ButtonRelease-1>", mousereleased, "+")
        self.bind("<Enter>", mouseenter)
        self.bind("<Leave>", mouseleave)
        self.winfo_toplevel().bind("<Escape>", cancel)
```

A navigation toolbar

In order to activate one-time rectangle zoom, we create a navigation toolbar in the app/toolkit/toolbars.py file that has to be connected to a MapView, and give it a button that simply turns on the one-time zoom mode of its connected MapView. While we are at it, we also create a toolbar button to zoom to the global bounding box of all of the layers in the MapView's layergroup. Remember to find and save icons for these two new buttons, zoom_rect.png and zoom_global.png. Refer to the following figure:

```
class NavigateTB(tk.Frame):
    def __init__(self, master, **kwargs):
        # get theme style
        style = style_toolbar_normal.copy()
        style.update(kwargs)

        # Make this class a subclass of tk.Frame and add to it
        tk.Frame.__init__(self, master, **style)

        # Modify some options
        self.config(width=80, height=40)

    def assign_mapview(self, mapview):
        mapview.navigation = self
        self.mapview = mapview

        # Add buttons
        self.global_view = IconButton(self, text="zoom global",
command=self.mapview.zoom_global)
        self.global_view.set_icon("zoom_global.png", width=32,
height=32)
        self.global_view.pack(side="left", padx=2, pady=2)
        self.zoom_rect = IconButton(self, text="zoom to
rectangle", command=self.mapview.zoom_rect)
        self.zoom_rect.set_icon("zoom_rect.png", width=32,
height=32)
        self.zoom_rect.pack(side="left", padx=2, pady=2)
```

The actual zooming calls to the renderer are defined as methods of the MapView widget, in `app/toolkit/map.py`:

```
    def zoom_global(self):
        layerbboxes = (layer.data.bbox for layer in
    self.renderer.layers)
        xmins,ymins,xmaxs,ymaxs = zip(*layerbboxes)
        globalbbox = [min(xmins), min(ymins), max(xmaxs),
    max(ymaxs)]
        self.renderer.zoom_bbox(*globalbbox)
        self.threaded_rendering()

    def zoom_rect(self):
        self.mouse_mode = "zoom"
        self.event_generate("<Enter>")

    def zoom_bbox(self, bbox):
        self.renderer.zoom_bbox(*bbox)
        self.threaded_rendering()
```

Putting it all together

We have now defined all of the necessary building blocks of a basic rendering application. These can be used and combined in many different ways. For instance, if you want to you can build an application that has a single LayerGroup/LayersPane connected with multiple independently zoomable MapViews, to view different locations of the same data simultaneously. In this book, we go for a more basic desktop GIS look.

Let's return to our GUI class that we created in *Chapter 3, Designing the Visual Look of Our Application,* and add more content to its startup phase. First we give the GUI a LayerGroup instance to hold our layers and link it to both the MapView and LayersPane widgets so they can communicate later on.

We also need a button to add data layers. There are many possible places to put such an important button, but for our current application, let's place it in the header of the LayersPane widget so that all things related to layers are kept logically grouped together. We want this button to have an icon, so let's first find and save a suitable icon as `add_layer.png` in the `app/icons` folder. Specifically, we want to create a button to add layers, assign it with our icon, and place it on the right side of the LayersPane header. When the button is clicked, it will run a `selectfiles` function, which opens a Tkinter file selection dialog window and adds all the selected files as new layers.

Loading data from a file may require that we specify the correct text encoding of the data. By default, we set it to utf8, but the user should be able to customize this and other data options in a separate data settings window. We store the data options dictionary as an attribute of the GUI class and allow it to be changed by user input in the settings window. This settings window is easily defined using our RunToolFrame template. To allow users to access this settings window, we add a data settings button right next to the add layer button. As usual, find and download an icon to use for the button, calling it data_options.png.

After that, let's create a ribbon tab for visualizing, giving it a button to save the contents of our MapView widget to an image file. Remember to find and save a save_image.png file, so we can give this button an icon. Finally, we add the navigation toolbar that we created earlier, hanging in the air in the upper part of the MapView.

Let's now add this new code to our GUI class' __init__ method, inside app/ builder.py:

```
        # Create a layergroup that keeps track of all the loaded
    data
        # ...so that all widgets can have access to the same data
        self.layers = pg.renderer.LayerGroup()

        # Assign layergroup to layerspane and mapview
        self.layerspane.assign_layergroup(self.layers)
        self.mapview.assign_layergroup(self.layers)

        ## Visualize tab
        visitab = self.ribbon.add_tab("Visualize")
        ### (Output toolbar)
        output = visitab.add_toolbar("Output")
        def save_image():
            filepath = asksaveasfilename()
            self.mapview.renderer.img.save(filepath)
        output.add_button(text="Save Image",
    icon="save_image.png",
                                command=save_image)

        # Place add layer button in the header of the layerspane
        def selectfiles():
            filepaths = askopenfilenames()
            for filepath in filepaths:
                encoding = self.data_options.get("encoding")
                self.layerspane.add_layer(filepath,
    encoding=encoding)
```

```
        button_addlayer = IconButton(self.layerspane.header,
command=selectfiles)
        button_addlayer.set_icon("add_layer.png", width=27,
height=27)
        button_addlayer.pack(side="right", anchor="e", ipadx=3,
padx=6, pady=3,)

        # Place button for setting data options
        self.data_options = {"encoding": "utf8"}
        button_data_options = IconButton(self.layerspane.header)
        button_data_options.set_icon("data_options.png", width=24,
height=21)
        button_data_options.pack(side="right", anchor="e",
ipadx=5, ipady=3, padx=6, pady=3,)

        # Open options window on button click
        def data_options_window():
            win = popups.RunToolWindow(self)

            # assign status bar
            win.assign_statusbar(self.statusbar)

            # place option input for data encoding
            win.add_option_input("Vector data encoding",
valuetype=str,
                                 argname="encoding",
default=self.data_options.get("encoding"))

            # when clicking OK, update data options
            def change_data_options(*args, **kwargs):
                """
                Customize settings for loading and saving data.

                Vector data encoding: Common options include
"utf8" or "latin"
                """
                # update user settings
                self.data_options.update(kwargs)

            def change_data_options_complete(result):
                # close window
                win.destroy()

            win.set_target_method("Changing data options",
change_data_options)
            win.set_finished_method(change_data_options_complete)
```

```
button_data_options["command"] = data_options_window

# Attach floating navigation toolbar inside mapwidget
self.navigation = NavigateTB(self.mapview)
self.navigation.place(relx=0.5, rely=0.03, anchor="n")
self.navigation.assign_mapview(self.mapview)
```

And that is about it! Your application should now be ready to use for rendering map data. Run `guitester.py`, and try to add some data and interact with the map. If you have done everything correctly, and, depending on your data, your screen should look something like this:

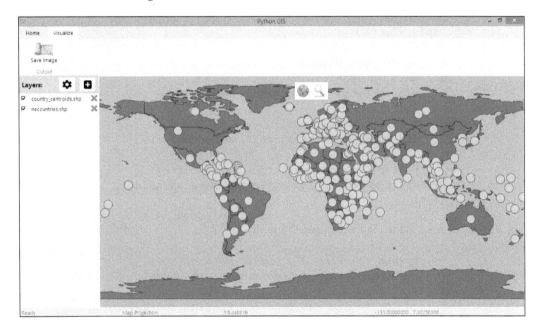

Summary

This chapter has been a fundamental milestone. We built a working geographic rendering module based on rearrangable layers in a LayerGroup, created a MapView widget for interactive displaying of these map renderings, made a visual LayersPane of the layers in our map, and enabled interactive zooming and panning of the MapView.

After following each step, you should now have what looks and feels like a GIS data inspecting application. Of course, a more sophisticated GIS needs additional methods not only to inspect data, but also to manage and edit data—which is what we turn to next.

5

Managing and Organizing Geographic Data

Now that we have an up-and-running explorative application, we can move on to developing some more day-to-day practical features. A common task for users of geographic data is to prepare, clean, restructure, and organize data. In this chapter, you will do the following:

- Create a window for inspecting the basic properties of each layer
- Build some convenience functions for commonly needed management tasks, and later add them to the user interface. These functions are as follows:
    - Operations on individual layers being available when the user right-clicks on each layer in the LayersPane widget (splitting, geometry cleaning, and resampling)
    - Batch operations on multiple layers available as buttons in the top ribbon area (merging and mosaicking)
- Assign dialogue windows to set the parameters when running each tool

Creating the management module

We start by creating a separate submodule to contain the functionality, one for vector, and one for raster. First, create the `vector/manager.py` file and start it up with the following imports:

```
import itertools, operator
from .data import *
```

Next, create the file `raster/manager.py` as follows:

```
import PIL, PIL.Image
```

To make these manager modules available to their respective `vector` and `raster` parent package, add the following import statement to both `vector/__init__.py` and `raster/__init__.py`:

```
import . import manager
```

Inspecting files

As the most basic way to organize and troubleshoot one's files, one often needs to inspect the properties and details of one's data and loaded layers. This information is usually available in a separate layer options window. Later in this chapter, we will make this window accessible by right-clicking on a layer, and clicking on **Properties** under the **Layer-specific right-click functions** subheading.

We define a template class for this type of window, with support for tabbed windows using our ribbon class, and create a convenience method for adding information in a nicely formatted way. This is done in the `app/dialogues.py` module. Since we have not yet set up the contents of `app/dialogues.py`, we also have to set up its imports and styling, as shown in the following code snippet:

```
import Tkinter as tk
import ScrolledText as tkst # a convenience module that ships with
Tkinter

from .toolkit.popups import *
from .toolkit.ribbon import *
from .toolkit import theme
from . import icons
from .. import vector, raster

style_layeroptions_info = {"fg": theme.font1["color"],
                           "font": theme.font1["type"],
                           "relief": "flat"}

class LayerOptionsWindow(Window):
    def __init__(self, master, **kwargs):
        # Make this class a subclass of tk.Menu and add to it
        Window.__init__(self, master, **kwargs)

        # Make the top ribbon selector
```

```
            self.ribbon = Ribbon(self)
            self.ribbon.pack(side="top", fill="both", expand=True)

    def add_info(self, tab, label, value):
        row = tk.Frame(tab, bg=tab.cget("bg"))
        row.pack(fill="x", anchor="n", pady=5, padx=5)

        # place label
        header = tk.Label(row, text=label, bg=tab.cget("bg"),
**style_layeroptions_info)
        header.pack(side="left", anchor="nw", padx=3)

        # place actual info text
        value = str(value)
        info = tk.Entry(row, width=400,
disabledbackground="white", justify="right",
**style_layeroptions_info)
        info.pack(side="right", anchor="ne", padx=3)
        info.insert(0, value)
        info.config(state="readonly")
        return info
```

Vector and raster data will typically have very different properties, so we make a separate window for each. First, for vector layers:

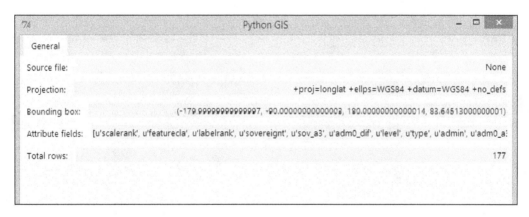

Here is the code for the same:

```
class VectorLayerOptionsWindow(LayerOptionsWindow):
    def __init__(self, master, layeritem, statusbar, **kwargs):
        # Make this class a subclass of tk.Menu and add to it
        LayerOptionsWindow.__init__(self, master, **kwargs)
        self.layeritem = layeritem
```

```
###########
### GENERAL OPTIONS TAB
general = self.ribbon.add_tab("General")

# add pieces of info
self.source = self.add_info(general, "Source file: ",
layeritem.renderlayer.data.filepath)
self.proj = self.add_info(general, "Projection: ",
self.layeritem.renderlayer.data.crs)
self.bbox = self.add_info(general, "Bounding box: ",
layeritem.renderlayer.data.bbox)
self.fields = self.add_info(general, "Attribute fields: ",
layeritem.renderlayer.data.fields)
self.rows = self.add_info(general, "Total rows: ",
len(layeritem.renderlayer.data))

###########
# Set starting tab
self.ribbon.switch(tabname="General")
```

Then, for raster layers:

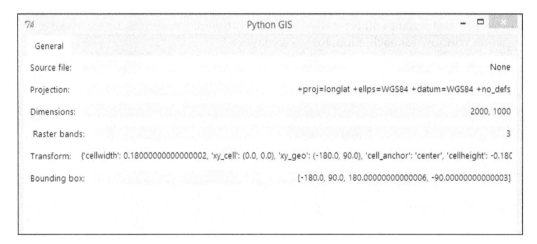

Here is the code for the same:

```
class RasterLayerOptionsWindow(LayerOptionsWindow):
    def __init__(self, master, layeritem, statusbar, **kwargs):
        # Make this class a subclass of tk.Menu and add to it
        LayerOptionsWindow.__init__(self, master, **kwargs)
        self.layeritem = layeritem
```

```
##########
### GENERAL OPTIONS TAB
general = self.ribbon.add_tab("General")

# add pieces of info
self.source = self.add_info(general, "Source file: ",
layeritem.renderlayer.data.filepath)
self.proj = self.add_info(general, "Projection: ",
self.layeritem.renderlayer.data.crs)
self.dims = self.add_info(general, "Dimensions: ", "%i,
%i"%(self.layeritem.renderlayer.data.width,

self.layeritem.renderlayer.data.height))
self.bands = self.add_info(general, " Raster bands: ",
"%i"%len(self.layeritem.renderlayer.data.bands))
self.transform = self.add_info(general, "Transform: ",
self.layeritem.renderlayer.data.info)
self.bbox = self.add_info(general, "Bounding box: ",
layeritem.renderlayer.data.bbox)

##########
# Set starting tab
self.ribbon.switch(tabname="General")
```

Organizing files

Traditionally, when working in a GIS application, one first seeks out the data files one wishes to use from various organizational websites. Ideally, one stores these in some logically organized folder structure on the local computer, and from there, one can load the data into the GIS application. In this section, we add functionality to help the user manage their files and access and alter basic file contents.

 For some great examples of the varied types and sources of GIS data available online, see the list at http://freegisdata.rtwilson.com/.

Vector data

Vector data is very versatile; its table-like data structure means that it can contain data on a wide variety of concepts in a single file, or contain data for only a very specific concept. For practical usage, it is easier if each file is tailored exactly to the data one needs, since these are represented as layers when loaded in the application. There are therefore many cases where the user may wish to reorganize the data to better fit their needs.

Here, we will implement three specific operations for organizing and maintaining vector data: splitting, merging, and cleaning. The following illustration gives a preview of the inputs and outputs of each:

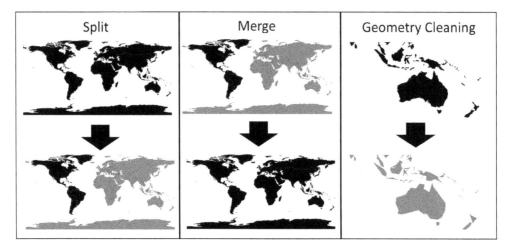

Splitting

For instance, the user may have a file that groups a diverse set of concepts, but is only interested in working with certain types separately. In such cases, it will be easier to just split the data for each unique occurrence of a field — known as splitting. In terms of data structure, this means slicing the height of the table into multiple tables along with their associated geometries. We do this conveniently using Python's built-in `sorted()` and `itertools groupby()` functions. A `splitfields` option defines a list of one or more field names to split on so that each unique value combination defines a new split. So, head to the `manager.py` file for vector data and write the following code:

```
def split(data, splitfields):
    fieldindexes = [index for index,field in
enumerate(data.fields)
                   if field in splitfields]
```

```
    sortedfeatures = sorted(data,
key=operator.itemgetter(*fieldindexes))
    grouped = itertools.groupby(sortedfeatures,
key=operator.itemgetter(*fieldindexes))
    for splitid,features in grouped:
        outfile = VectorData()
        outfile.fields = list(data.fields)
        for oldfeat in features:
            outfile.add_feature(oldfeat.row, oldfeat.geometry)
        yield outfile
```

Merging

One can also face the opposite scenario, where one wishes to group together a series of data files spread across multiple files. This is called a **merge operation**. A merge operation stacks the rows from multiple tables into one big one, and generally increases the spatial coverage, since it leads to a bigger collection of geometries. The output attribute table from this operation also expands horizontally to include all of the variables/fields from its input files. Finally, remember that the VectorData instances can only contain one type of geometry (points, lines, or polygons), so trying to merge layers of different geometry types will result in an error. We implement it in the following way:

```
def merge(*datalist):
    #make empty table
    firstfile = datalist[0]
    outfile = VectorData()
    #combine fields from all files
    outfields = list(firstfile.fields)
    for data in datalist[1:]:
        for field in data.fields:
            if field not in outfields:
                outfields.append(field)
    outfile.fields = outfields
    #add the rest of the files
    for data in datalist:
        for feature in data:
            geometry = feature.geometry.copy()
            row = []
            for field in outfile.fields:
                if field in data.fields:
                    row.append( feature[field] )
                else:
                    row.append( "" )
```

```
                    outfile.add_feature(row, geometry)
        #return merged file
        return outfile
```

Geometry cleaning

Geographic data can come from a very wide variety of sources, and this means that their levels of integrity can vary greatly. For instance, there are many rules that govern what is and is not allowed for each geometry type, but not all data producers (including both software and individuals) use the same rules or follow them to the same degree. This can be a problem for GIS processing, analysis applications, and programming libraries if the data is corrupted or not formatted in the way that is expected. Data may also contain unnecessary junk information that doesn't add anything useful (depending on the level of detail needed), making the file size overly large. Geometry cleaning can therefore be a useful feature as a first step when gathering one's data.

To do this, we make a function that loops the geometries of our features. With the help of the Shapely library, we fix "bowtie" errors (polygons only), remove repeat points, and exclude any remaining geometries deemed to be invalid according to the GeoJSON specification. The tolerance argument can be set to higher than zero to reduce file size, but note that this alters the shape of the geometries and decreases the level of detail and precision in the output. Refer to the following code:

```
def clean(data, tolerance=0):
    # create new file
    outfile = VectorData()
    outfile.fields = list(data.fields)

    # clean
    for feat in data:
        shapelyobj = feat.get_shapely()

        # try fixing invalid geoms
        if not shapelyobj.is_valid:
            if "Polygon" in shapelyobj.type:
                # fix bowtie polygons
                shapelyobj = shapelyobj.buffer(0.0)

        # remove repeat points (tolerance=0)
        # (and optionally smooth out complex shapes, tolerance >
0)
        shapelyobj = shapelyobj.simplify(tolerance)
```

```
# if still invalid, do not add to output
if not shapelyobj.is_valid:
    continue

# write to file
geojson = shapelyobj.__geo_interface__
outfile.add_feature(feat.row, geojson)

return outfile
```

For more on polygon bowtie errors, visit:
http://stackoverflow.com/questions/20833344/
fix-invalid-polygon-python-shapely

Raster data

There are many common raster file management functionalities that you may wish to implement. Here, we will only focus on two of them: mosaicking and resampling, as seen in the following screenshot:

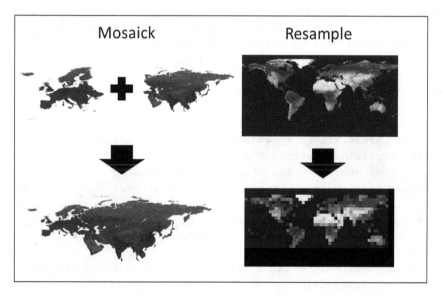

To implement these functionalities, we will take advantage of the image processing functionality from the PIL library. Since we are using an imaging library not primarily intended for geospatial data, the following code should be considered highly experimental and mostly for demonstration purposes; you may have to troubleshoot and improve on these methods on your own.

If the main purpose of your application is to process satellite, imagery, and raster data, and you don't have time or feel comfortable finding your own solution using PIL, you may be better off just adding NumPy, GDAL, and related tools as dependencies.

For a list of GDAL's broad range of functionality for handling raster data, see:

https://pcjericks.github.io/py-gdalogr-cookbook/

Mosaicking

Similar to how vector data can be merged together, it is also possible to mosaic multiple adjacent raster datasets into a single larger raster data. The way we implement it here is by creating an align_rasters() function, which takes any number of rasters, automatically finds the coordinate bounding box that contains all, as well as the required pixel dimensions (though we should probably allow some user control here), and uses this information to position each raster to their respective location in a region that bounds all of our rasters. We add this as a function in the raster/manager.py file:

```
def align_rasters(*rasters):
    "Used internally by other functions only, not by user"
    # get coord bbox containing all rasters
    for rast in rasters: print rast.bbox
    xlefts,ytops,xrights,ybottoms = zip(*[rast.bbox for rast in
rasters])
    if xlefts[0] < xrights[0]:
        xleft,xright = min(xlefts),max(xrights)
    else: xleft,xright = max(xlefts),min(xrights)
    if ytops[0] > ybottoms[0]:
        ytop,ybottom = max(ytops),min(ybottoms)
    else: ytop,ybottom = min(ytops),max(ybottoms)

    # get the required pixel dimensions (based on first raster,
but should probably allow user to specify)
    xs,ys = (xleft,xright),(ytop,ybottom)
    coordwidth,coordheight = max(xs)-min(xs), max(ys)-min(ys)
    rast = rasters[0]
    orig_xs,orig_ys =
(rast.bbox[0],rast.bbox[2]),(rast.bbox[1],rast.bbox[3])
    orig_coordwidth,orig_coordheight = max(orig_xs)-min(orig_xs),
max(orig_ys)-min(orig_ys)
    widthratio,heightratio = coordwidth/orig_coordwidth,
coordheight/orig_coordheight
```

```
reqwidth = int(round(rast.width*widthratio))
reqheight = int(round(rast.height*heightratio))

# position into same coordbbox
aligned = []
for rast in rasters:
    coordbbox = [xleft,ytop,xright,ybottom]
    positioned = rast.positioned(reqwidth, reqheight,
coordbbox)
    aligned.append(positioned)
return aligned
```

Since we now have a way to align and properly position the rasters in space, we can easily mosaic them into a new raster by simply creating a new grid with dimensions that bound all rasters and pasting each raster into it:

```
def mosaic(*rasters):
    """
    Mosaic rasters covering different areas together into one
file.
    Parts of the rasters may overlap each other, in which case we
use the value
    from the last listed raster (the "last" overlap rule).
    """
    # align all rasters, ie resampling to the same dimensions as
the first raster
    aligned = align_rasters(*rasters)
    # copy the first raster and reset the cached mask for the new
raster
    firstalign,firstmask = aligned[0]
    merged = firstalign.copy()
    del merged._cached_mask
    # paste onto each other, ie "last" overlap rule
    for rast,mask in aligned[1:]:
        merged.bands[0].img.paste(rast.bands[0].img, (0,0), mask)

    return merged
```

Note that unlike a vector merge, where overlapping geometries are kept in their original form, raster mosaicking needs a rule for choosing a value when there are overlapping cells. In the previous code, we didn't support any customization of the overlap rule, but instead just pasted each raster on top of each other so that any overlapping cells hold the value of the last raster to be pasted-a so-called "last" rule. You may implement other overlap-rules by looking at the tools available in the PIL library, such as average value with `PIL.Image.blend()`, or min or max with the functions found in the `PIL.ImageOps` submodule.

Resampling

For raster data, the equivalent to vector cleaning is the removal of unnecessary detail and file size reduction, which can be done by resampling the size and frequency of the grid cells. Such resampling involves algorithms for smoothing out and redistributing the old cell values to the new cell structure. A lot of the same principles apply to resizing an image. Fortunately for us, our raster data values are stored in a PIL Image class, so we simply use its resize method with the nearest neighbor algorithm, which asks for a size in terms of pixels (or number of grid cells in our case). For the convenience of the user, we also give them the alternative to, instead specify the desired geographic width and height of each cell (for instance, degrees or meters, depending on the data's coordinate reference system), with our program calculating the necessary grid resolution behind the scenes. If specified, remember that the *y* axis of geographic coordinates tend to run in the opposite direction to that of raster coordinates, so cellheight must be given as a negative number. If the user is curious about the grid dimensions or cell size of their existing raster, remember that this can be found in the layer properties window we created earlier this chapter.

An alternative library for raster resampling here will be PyResample. I chose not to use it in our lightweight application due to its NumPy and SciPy dependence.

Other useful libraries for raster management functionality that you may wish to explore are GDAL as mentioned earlier or Rasterio which depends on GDAL.

Take a look at the following code:

```
def resample(raster, width=None, height=None, cellwidth=None,
cellheight=None):
    raster = raster.copy()

    if width and height:
        # calculate new cell dimensions based on the new raster
size
        widthfactor = raster.width / float(width)
        heightfactor = raster.height / float(height)
        oldcellwidth, oldcellheight = raster.info["cellwidth"],
raster.info["cellheight"]
        newcellwidth, newcellheight = oldcellwidth * widthfactor,
oldcellheight * heightfactor
```

```
        # resample each grid
        for band in raster:
            band.img = band.img.resize((width, height),
PIL.Image.NEAREST)
            # update cells access
            band.cells = band.img.load()

        # remember new celldimensions
        raster.info["cellwidth"] = newcellwidth
        raster.info["cellheight"] = newcellheight
        return raster

    elif cellwidth and cellheight:
        # calculate new raster size based on the new cell
dimensions
        widthfactor = raster.info["cellwidth"] / float(cellwidth)
        heightfactor = raster.info["cellheight"] /
float(cellheight)
        oldwidth, oldheight = raster.width, raster.height
        newwidth, newheight = int(round(oldwidth * widthfactor)),
int(round(oldheight * heightfactor))

        # resample each grid
        for band in raster:
            band.img = band.img.resize((newwidth, newheight),
PIL.Image.NEAREST)
            # update cells access
            band.cells = band.img.load()

        # remember new celldimensions
        raster.info["cellwidth"] = cellwidth
        raster.info["cellheight"] = cellheight
        return raster

    else:
        raise Exception("To rescale raster, either width and
height or cellwidth and cellheight must be specified.")
```

Weaving functionality into the user interface

Now, we get to the part where we can make the management functionality created earlier accessible to the user in the visual user interface.

Layer-specific right-click functions

Some of the functionality we created in this chapter is intrinsically bound to only one layer, so it makes sense to make these available directly by right-clicking on the desired layer to operate on. Such a feature is only specific to the application we are currently making, so let's define this right-click menu in the app/dialogues. py module. Since Tkinter already has such a nicely formatted popup menu widget, with easy methods for adding items and commands, all we need to do is subclass it. Vector and raster layers will each get their own menu, but both will have in common items called as **Rename**, **Save as**, and **Properties**. To give them better visuals, find the three .png images with the same names as each of these items so we can assign them to the menu items, saving them inside the app/icons folder.

First, we make the options menu for vector layers. We give it the split and clean functions we created earlier, and assign them icons, which you must find and save as app/icons/split.png and app/icons/clean.png. Refer to the following screenshot:

```
class RightClickMenu_VectorLayer(tk.Menu):
    def __init__(self, master, layerspane, layeritem, statusbar,
**kwargs):
        # Make this class a subclass of tk.Menu and add to it
        tk.Menu.__init__(self, master, tearoff=0, **kwargs)
        self.layerspane = layerspane
        self.layeritem = layeritem
```

```
        self.statusbar = statusbar
        self.imgs = dict()

        # Renaming
        self.imgs["rename"] = icons.get("rename.png", width=32,
height=32)
        self.add_command(label="Rename",
command=self.layeritem.ask_rename, image=self.imgs["rename"],
compound="left")

        # Saving
        def ask_save():
            savepath = asksaveasfilename()
            self.statusbar.task.start("Saving layer to file...")
            pending =
dispatch.request_results(self.layeritem.renderlayer.data.save,
args=[savepath])
            def finish(result):
                if isinstance(result, Exception):
                    popup_message(self, str(result) + "\n\n" +
savepath)
                self.statusbar.task.stop()
            dispatch.after_completion(self, pending, finish)
        self.imgs["save"] = icons.get("save.png", width=32,
height=32)
        self.add_command(label="Save as", command=ask_save,
image=self.imgs["save"], compound="left")

        # ---(Breakline)---
        self.add_separator()

        # Splitting
        def open_options_window():
            window = VectorSplitOptionWindow(self.layeritem,
self.layerspane, self.layeritem, statusbar)
        self.imgs["split"] = icons.get("split.png", width=32,
height=32)
        self.add_command(label="Split to layers",
command=open_options_window, image=self.imgs["split"],
compound="left")

        # ---(Breakline)---
        self.add_separator()

        # Cleaning
```

```
        def open_options_window():
            window = VectorCleanOptionWindow(self.layeritem,
    self.layerspane, self.layeritem, statusbar)
            self.imgs["clean"] = icons.get("clean.png", width=32,
    height=32)
            self.add_command(label="Clean Geometries",
    command=open_options_window, image=self.imgs["clean"],
    compound="left")

        # ---(Breakline)---
        self.add_separator()

        # View properties
        def view_properties():
            window = VectorLayerOptionsWindow(self.layeritem,
    self.layeritem, statusbar)
            self.imgs["properties"] = icons.get("properties.png",
    width=32, height=32)
            self.add_command(label="Properties",
    command=view_properties, image=self.imgs["properties"],
    compound="left")
```

We then move onto the options menu for rasters layers. The only layer-specific function here is resample(), so find and save an icon for it as app/icons/resample.png. You can see an icon named **Resample** in the following screenshot:

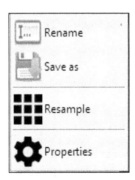

Refer to the following code:

```
class RightClickMenu_RasterLayer(tk.Menu):
    def __init__(self, master, layerspane, layeritem, statusbar,
    **kwargs):
        # Make this class a subclass of tk.Menu and add to it
        tk.Menu.__init__(self, master, tearoff=0, **kwargs)
        self.layerspane = layerspane
```

```
        self.layeritem = layeritem
        self.statusbar = statusbar
        self.imgs = dict()

        # Renaming
        self.imgs["rename"] = icons.get("rename.png", width=32,
height=32)
        self.add_command(label="Rename",
command=self.layeritem.ask_rename, image=self.imgs["rename"],
compound="left")

        # Saving
        def ask_save():
            savepath = asksaveasfilename()
            self.statusbar.task.start("Saving layer to file...")
            pending =
dispatch.request_results(self.layeritem.renderlayer.data.save,
args=[savepath])
            def finish(result):
                if isinstance(result, Exception):
                    popup_message(self, str(result) + "\n\n" +
savepath)
                self.statusbar.task.stop()
            dispatch.after_completion(self, pending, finish)
        self.imgs["save"] = icons.get("save.png", width=32,
height=32)
        self.add_command(label="Save as", command=ask_save,
image=self.imgs["save"], compound="left")

        # ---(Breakline)---
        self.add_separator()

        # Resampling
        def open_options_window():
            window = RasterResampleOptionWindow(self.layeritem,
self.layerspane, self.layeritem, statusbar)
        self.imgs["resample"] = icons.get("resample.png",
width=32, height=32)
        self.add_command(label="Resample",
command=open_options_window, image=self.imgs["resample"],
compound="left")

        # ---(Breakline)---
        self.add_separator()
```

```
        # View properties
        def view_properties():
            window = RasterLayerOptionsWindow(self.layeritem,
    self.layeritem, statusbar)
            self.imgs["properties"] = icons.get("properties.png",
    width=32, height=32)
            self.add_command(label="Properties",
    command=view_properties, image=self.imgs["properties"],
    compound="left")
```

Defining the tool options windows

In the preceding code, clicking on an item in the menu opens an options window for a specific tool. We will now create these options windows in app/dialogues. py, utilizing our helpful RunToolFrame template to populate the window with appropriate options and widgets. Since these are layer-specific tools, we also remember to set the layer data as a hidden argument. Finally, the results from the processes are added to our LayersPane. The following screenshot shows the options window for vector cleaning:

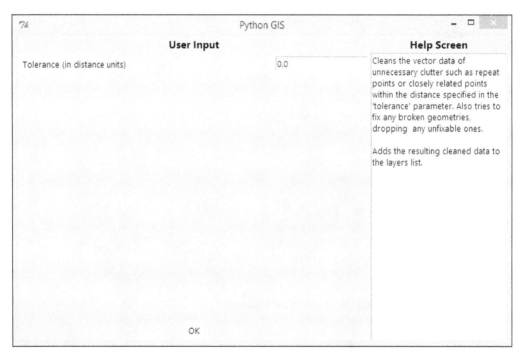

Here is the code to implement the mentioned functionality:

```
class VectorCleanOptionWindow(Window):
    def __init__(self, master, layerspane, layeritem, statusbar,
**kwargs):
        # Make this class a subclass and add to it
        Window.__init__(self, master, **kwargs)

        # Create runtoolframe
        self.runtool = RunToolFrame(self)
        self.runtool.pack(fill="both", expand=True)
        self.runtool.assign_statusbar(statusbar)

        # Add a hidden option from its associated layeritem data
        self.runtool.add_hidden_option(argname="data",
value=layeritem.renderlayer.data)

        # Set the remaining options
        self.runtool.set_target_method("Cleaning data...",
vector.manager.clean)
        self.runtool.add_option_input(argname="tolerance",
label="Tolerance (in distance units)",
                                      valuetype=float, default=0.0,
minval=0.0, maxval=1.0)

        # Define how to process
        newname = layeritem.namelabel["text"] + "_cleaned"
        def process(result):
            if isinstance(result, Exception):
                popup_message(self, "Failed to clean the data:" +
"\n\n" + str(result) )
            else:
                layerspane.add_layer(result, name=newname)
                self.destroy()

        self.runtool.set_finished_method(process)
```

The following screenshot demonstrates the options window for vector splitting populated with a list of field to choose from:

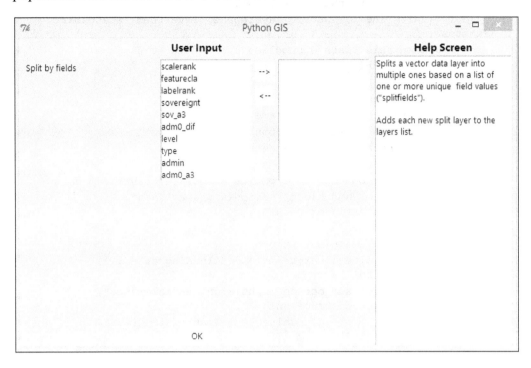

Here is the code to implement the mentioned functionality:

```
class VectorSplitOptionWindow(Window):
    def __init__(self, master, layerspane, layeritem, statusbar,
**kwargs):
        # Make this class a subclass and add to it
        Window.__init__(self, master, **kwargs)

        # Create runtoolframe
        self.runtool = RunToolFrame(self)
        self.runtool.pack(fill="both", expand=True)
        self.runtool.assign_statusbar(statusbar)

        # Add a hidden option from its associated layeritem data
        self.runtool.add_hidden_option(argname="data",
value=layeritem.renderlayer.data)

        # Set the remaining options
        self.runtool.set_target_method("Splitting data...",
vector.manager.split)
```

```
self.runtool.add_option_input(argname="splitfields",
                            label="Split by fields",
                            multi=True,
        choices=layeritem.renderlayer.data.fields,
                            valuetype=str)


        # Define how to process
        def process(result):
            if isinstance(result, Exception):
                popup_message(self, "Failed to split the data:" +
"\n\n" + str(result) )
            else:
                for splitdata in result:
                    layerspane.add_layer(splitdata)
                    self.update()
                self.destroy()
        self.runtool.set_finished_method(process)
```

As shown in the following screenshot of the raster resampling window a user can manually enter input for height and width of raster and cell data:

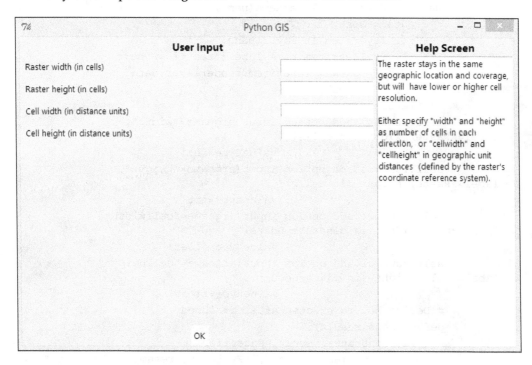

Here is the code for same:

```
class RasterResampleOptionWindow(Window):
    def __init__(self, master, layerspane, layeritem, statusbar,
**kwargs):
        # Make this class a subclass and add to it
        Window.__init__(self, master, **kwargs)

        # Create runtoolframe
        self.runtool = RunToolFrame(self)
        self.runtool.pack(fill="both", expand=True)
        self.runtool.assign_statusbar(statusbar)

        # Add a hidden option from its associated layeritem data
        self.runtool.add_hidden_option(argname="raster",
value=layeritem.renderlayer.data)

        # Set the remaining options
        self.runtool.set_target_method("Resampling data...",
raster.manager.resample)
        def get_data_from_layername(name):
            data = None
            for layeritem in layerspane:
                if layeritem.name_label["text"] == name:
                    data = layeritem.renderlayer.data
                    break
            return data
        self.runtool.add_option_input(argname="width",
label="Raster width (in cells)",
                                      valuetype=int)
        self.runtool.add_option_input(argname="height",
label="Raster height (in cells)",
                                      valuetype=int)
        self.runtool.add_option_input(argname="cellwidth",
label="Cell width (in distance units)",
                                      valuetype=float)
        self.runtool.add_option_input(argname="cellheight",
label="Cell height (in distance units)",
                                      valuetype=float)
        # Define how to process after finished
        def process(result):
            if isinstance(result, Exception):
                popup_message(self, "Failed to resample the data:"
+ "\n\n" + str(result) )
            else:
```

```
                layerspane.add_layer(result)
                self.destroy()
        self.runtool.set_finished_method(process)
```

Finally, we need to instruct our application that right-clicking on a layer should open the appropriate menu. We define this in the initialization phase of the class defining our GUI in our app/builder.py module, after creating the LayersPane:

```
        # Bind layeritem right click behavior
        def layer_rightclick(event):
            layeritem = event.widget.master.master
            if isinstance(layeritem.renderlayer,
    pg.renderer.VectorLayer):
                menu = RightClickMenu_VectorLayer(self,
    self.layerspane, layeritem, self.statusbar)
            elif isinstance(layeritem.renderlayer,
    pg.renderer.RasterLayer):
                menu = RightClickMenu_RasterLayer(self,
    self.layerspane, layeritem, self.statusbar)
            # Place and show menu
            menu.post(event.x_root, event.y_root)
        self.layerspane.bind_layer_rightclick(layer_rightclick)
```

Setting up the management tab

In contrast to the right-click menu of individual layers, the top ribbon tabs should be reserved for more general functionalities that takes multiple layers as input.

All of our data management-related functionality goes in a separate tab called **Manage**, to which we attach a vector and a raster toolbar, each populated with one or more buttons that open an options window for running related functionalities. Therefore, we add the following to app/builder.py in our GUI class after having created the ribbon and the visualize tab, as shown in the following screenshot:

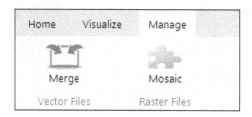

Here is the code to set up the **Manage** tab:

```
## Management tab
managetab = self.ribbon.add_tab("Manage")
### (Vector toolbar)
vectorfiles = managetab.add_toolbar("Vector Files")
def open_merge_window():
    window = VectorMergeOptionWindow(self,
self.layerspane, self.statusbar)
    vectorfiles.add_button(text="Merge",
icon="vector_merge.png",
                            command=open_merge_window)
### (Raster toolbar)
rasterfiles = managetab.add_toolbar("Raster Files")
def open_mosaic_window():
    window = RasterMosaicOptionWindow(self,
self.layerspane, self.statusbar)
    rasterfiles.add_button(text="Mosaic", icon="mosaic.png",
                            command=open_mosaic_window)
```

Defining the tool options windows

We define the various tool-specific options windows in app/dialogues.py, as we did earlier in text. First for the vector merge tool window, as seen in the following screenshot:

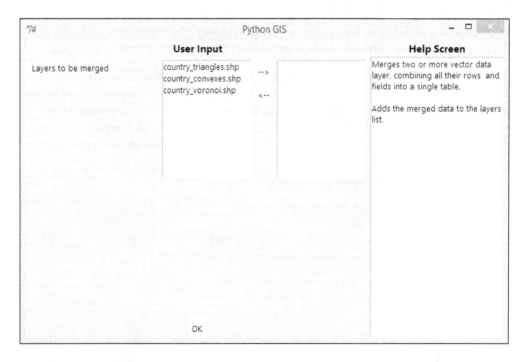

Here is the code for same:

```
class VectorMergeOptionWindow(Window):
    def __init__(self, master, layerspane, statusbar, **kwargs):
        # Make this class a subclass and add to it
        Window.__init__(self, master, **kwargs)

        # Create runtoolframe
        self.runtool = RunToolFrame(self)
        self.runtool.pack(fill="both", expand=True)
        self.runtool.assign_statusbar(statusbar)

        # Set the remaining options
        self.runtool.set_target_method("Merging data...",
vector.manager.merge)
        def get_data_from_layername(name):
            data = None
            for layeritem in layerspane:
                if layeritem.namelabel["text"] == name:
                    data = layeritem.renderlayer.data
                    break
            return data
        self.runtool.add_option_input(argname=None,
                            label="Layers to be merged",
                            multi=True,
                            choices=[layeritem.namelabel["text"]
for layeritem in layerspane],
                            valuetype=get_data_from_layername)

        # Define how to process
        def process(result):
            if isinstance(result, Exception):
                popup_message(self, "Failed to merge the data:" +
"\n\n" + str(result) )
```

```
        else:
            layerspane.add_layer(result, name="merged")
        self.runtool.set_finished_method(process)
```

The options window for the raster mosaicking tool looks as follows:

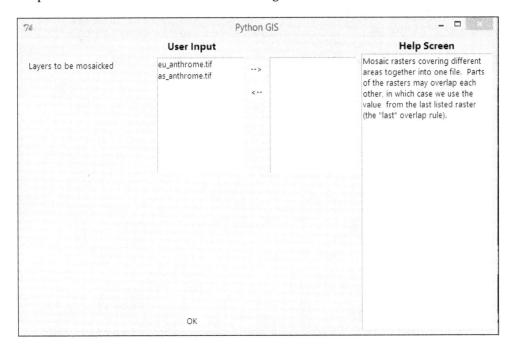

Here is the code:

```
class RasterMosaicOptionWindow(Window):
    def __init__(self, master, layerspane, statusbar, **kwargs):
        # Make this class a subclass and add to it
        Window.__init__(self, master, **kwargs)

        # Create runtoolframe
        self.runtool = RunToolFrame(self)
        self.runtool.pack(fill="both", expand=True)
        self.runtool.assign_statusbar(statusbar)

        # Set the remaining options
        self.runtool.set_target_method("Mosaicking data...",
raster.manager.mosaic)
        def get_data_from_layername(name):
            data = None
            for layeritem in layerspane:
```

```
            if layeritem.namelabel["text"] == name:
                data = layeritem.renderlayer.data
                break
        return data
    self.runtool.add_option_input(argname=None,
                        label="Layers to be mosaicked",
                        multi=True,
                        choices=[layeritem.namelabel["text"]
for layeritem in layerspane],
                        valuetype=get_data_from_layername)


    # Define how to process
    def process(result):
        if isinstance(result, Exception):
            popup_message(self, "Failed to mosaick the data:"
+ "\n\n" + str(result) )
        else:
            layerspane.add_layer(result, name="mosaicked")
    self.runtool.set_finished_method(process)
```

Summary

In this chapter, we created functionalities related to managing and organizing files. This included a window to inspect the basic properties of any data layer. As for operations, we implemented splitting, merging, and geometry cleaning for vector data, and mosaicking and resampling for raster data. These functions were then made available in the application GUI, some by choosing from a pop-up menu when right-clicking on a layer, others by clicking on an icon button in the management tab up by the top ribbon. Each tool got its own window dialogue class with editable options.

By going through this chapter, you should now know the general steps involved in adding a geospatial functionality, making it accessible in the GUI, and adding the results as a new layer if desired. As we move on to the next chapter, where we will build some basic analysis functionality, all we need to do is repeat and follow the same steps and procedures.

6
Analyzing Geographic Data

At some point, after acquiring, preparing, and organizing data to fit your needs, you eventually get to the point where you can actually use this data for some greater good: to form queries, explore, answer questions, test hypotheses, and so on. In this chapter, you will develop some of these capabilities along with their application components, specifically:

- Create the analysis functionality:
    - Overlay summary and distance buffer for vector data
    - Zonal summary statistics for raster data
- Add ways to access them through the user interface

Creating the analysis module

We start by creating what we will call the `app/analyzer.py` module with the necessary imports. One in the `vector` folder:

```
import itertools, operator
from .data import *

import shapely
from shapely.prepared import prep as supershapely
```

And one in the `raster` folder:

```
import itertools, operator
from .data import *
from .manager import *

import PIL.Image, PIL.ImageMath, PIL.ImageStat
```

As usual, we must make these new modules importable from their parent packages, to add the following import statement in both `vector/__init__.py` and `raster/__init__.py`:

```
from . import analyzer
```

Analyzing data

The first half of this chapter creates the analysis functionality, while the other half weaves the functionality into the application design. Let's begin by making the functionality. This includes overlap summary and buffer for vector data and zonal statistics for raster data.

Vector data

For vector data, we will focus on two commonly used analysis tools: overlap summary and buffer.

Overlap summary

One of the most basic spatial analysis operations in a GIS is to summarize statistics for a layer of features that touches or overlaps another layer of features. Typical questions to warrant such analysis include: how many points fall within each country polygon, or what is the sum or average of their values for each country? This type of analysis is typically done using a *spatial join* tool, with the many-to-one option representing multiple matching features with a summary statistic. These summary statistics are then attached to the original country polygons. A spatial join is not an analysis in itself, it just does the number crunching that the user can later use to analyze, for instance, visually on a map or in a table graph. In my experience, this is one of the most common reasons for using spatial joins, as a preprocessing step, but it is still a crucial part of overlay analysis.

The following screenshot shows a typical way that overlay analysis can be used to aggregate values and visualize patterns:

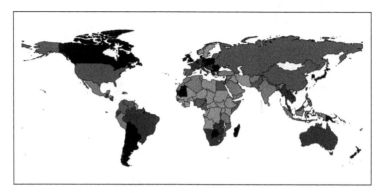

Since our application is geared more toward less technical users, and we want to make everything as obvious as possible, we make this particular usage of spatial join into a tool of its own and give it a name that more appropriately describes the analysis end product: overlap summary. The tool has been assigned the data, to group the statistics into the data, containing the values that will be summarized, and a list of fieldname statistic tuples to be calculated in the output, also known as a **fieldmapping**. Valid statistic values are count, sum, max, min, and average. As an example of a fieldmapping, this tool expects that if we want the output file to calculate the count of major cities and the sum of their populations, we will write it as `[("city_id", "count"), ("city_pop", "sum")]`. Note that the fieldmapping follows the usual Python syntax with strings having quote marks around them, which is also how we input them through the user interface later in text. For detecting overlap, we use the Shapely module's `intersects` operation. Also note that the use of Shapely's less known `prep` function (imported as `supershapely`) gives incredible speedups for multiple repeated intersect comparisons on the same geometry.

So, head into `vector/analyzer.py` and add the following function:

```
def overlap_summary(groupbydata, valuedata, fieldmapping=[]):
    # prep
    data1,data2 = groupbydata,valuedata
    if fieldmapping: aggfields,aggtypes = zip(*fieldmapping)
    aggfunctions = dict([("count",len),
                         ("sum",sum),
                         ("max",max),
                         ("min",min),
                         ("average",lambda seq:
sum(seq)/float(len(seq)) ) ])
```

```
# create spatial index
if not hasattr(data1, "spindex"): data1.create_spatial_index()
if not hasattr(data2, "spindex"): data2.create_spatial_index()

# create new
new = VectorData()
new.fields = list(data1.fields)
if fieldmapping:
    for aggfield,aggtype in fieldmapping:
        new.fields.append(aggfield)

# for each groupby feature
for i,feat in enumerate(data1.quick_overlap(data2.bbox)):
    geom = feat.get_shapely()
    geom = supershapely(geom)
    matches = []

    # get all value features that intersect
    for otherfeat in data2.quick_overlap(feat.bbox):
        othergeom = otherfeat.get_shapely()
        if geom.intersects(othergeom):
            matches.append(otherfeat)

    # make newrow from original row
    newrow = list(feat.row)

    # if any matches
    if matches:
        def make_number(value):
            try: return float(value)
            except: return None

        # add summary values to newrow based on fieldmapping
        for aggfield,aggtype in fieldmapping:
            values = [otherfeat[aggfield] for otherfeat in
matches]
            if aggtype in ("sum","max","min","average"):
                # only consider number values if numeric stats
                values = [make_number(value) for value in
values if make_number(value) != None]
            aggregatefunc = aggfunctions[aggtype]
            summaryvalue = aggregatefunc(values)
            newrow.append(summaryvalue)
```

```
    # otherwise, add empty values
    else:
        newrow.extend(("" for _ in fieldmapping))

    # write feature to output
    new.add_feature(newrow, feat.geometry)

return new
```

Buffer

If, in your analysis, you also want to include features that don't necessarily overlap the grouping features but are within a certain distance, then buffering is a good tool to use. A buffer operation is one where a geometric feature is grown or shrunk by a specified distance. After expanding the geometries to the desired distance, one can then follow up with the previously implemented overlap summary tool and, this way, also include near-overlap features in the statistics. Refer to the following screenshot to see an example of a polygon buffer operation:

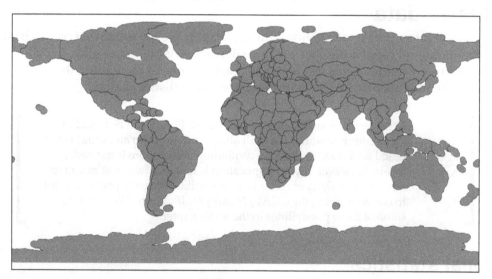

We implement this quite simply with Shapely's `buffer` method, with positive numbers for growing and negative numbers for shrinking. To make it a bit more interesting, we let the user dynamically set the buffer distance based on an expression. The expression should take the form of a string representing Python code, referencing the feature as **feat**, which allows buffering based on one or more of its attributes or even math expressions. For instance, to buffer a layer of countries based on GDP per capita and scaled down for visibility, we may write something like: *(feat['GDP'] / float(feat['population'])) / 500.0.*

Inside `vector/analyzer.py`, add the following code:

```
def buffer(data, dist_expression):
    # buffer and change each geojson dict in-place
    new = VectorData()
    new.fields = list(data.fields)
    for feat in data:
        geom = feat.get_shapely()
        dist = eval(dist_expression)
        buffered = geom.buffer(dist)
        if not buffered.is_empty:
            geojson = buffered.__geo_interface__
            geojson["type"] = buffered.type
            new.add_feature(feat.row, geojson)
    # change data type to polygon
    new.type = "Polygon"
    return new
```

Raster data

To analyze raster data in our lightweight application, we are somewhat constrained by the speed and capabilities that our main dependency PIL has to offer. Luckily, there are many hidden gems inside the PIL package, one of them being the `ImageStat` module that we use to implement zonal statistics analysis.

> Other useful functionalities from the PIL library can be found in its `ImageMath` module. This will allow us to produce an output raster based on a math expression combining one or more input raster layers. However, if your application is first and foremost meant for advanced analysis of raster data or satellite imagery, you may want to consider going the GDAL/NumPy/SciPy route. We return to some of these possibilities in the final chapter.

Zonal statistics

Zonal statistics is a common GIS tool that takes each category or zone from one raster and summarizes the values of overlapping cells from another raster. In a sense, zonal statistics is the raster equivalent of overlap summary. In our implementation, we return both a dictionary containing various statistics for each zone and a copy of the zonal raster, where the value for each zone is based on one of its global summary statistics. The user must specify which band from the zonal and value data to use, and set the outstat statistics option to one of: `mean`, `median`, `max`, `min`, `stdev`, `var`, `count`, or `sum`.

Inside `raster/analyser.py` write:

```python
def zonal_statistics(zonaldata, valuedata, zonalband=0,
valueband=0, outstat="mean"):
    """
    For each unique zone in "zonaldata", summarizes "valuedata"
    cells that overlap "zonaldata".
    Which band to use must be specified for each.

    The "outstat" statistics option can be one of: mean, median,
    max, min, stdev, var, count, or sum
    """
    # get nullvalues
    nullzone = zonaldata.info.get("nodata_value")

    # position value grid into zonal grid
    (valuedata,valuemask) = valuedata.positioned(zonaldata.width,
    zonaldata.height,

                                                  zonaldata.bbox)

    # pick one image band for each
    zonalimg = zonaldata.bands[zonalband].img
    valueimg = valuedata.bands[valueband].img

    # create output image, using nullzone as nullvalue
    outimg = PIL.Image.new("F", zonalimg.size, nullzone)

    # get stats for each unique value in zonal data
    zonevalues = [val for count,val in zonalimg.getcolors()]
    zonesdict = {}
    for zoneval in zonevalues:
        # exclude nullzone
        if zoneval == nullzone: continue

        # mask only the current zone
        zonemask = zonalimg.point(lambda px: 1 if px == zoneval
else 0, "1")
        fullmask = PIL.Image.new("1", zonemask.size, 0)
        # also exclude null values from calculations
        fullmask.paste(zonemask, valuemask)

        # retrieve stats
        stats = PIL.ImageStat.Stat(valueimg, fullmask)
        statsdict = {}
        statsdict["min"],statsdict["max"] = stats.extrema[0]
```

```
        for stattype in
("count","sum","mean","median","var","stddev"):
            try: statsdict[stattype] =
stats.__getattr__(stattype)[0]
            except ZeroDivisionError: statsdict[stattype] = None
        zonesdict[zoneval] = statsdict

        # write chosen stat to outimg
        outimg.paste(statsdict[outstat], (0,0), zonemask)

    # make outimg to raster
    outraster = Raster(image=outimg, **zonaldata.info)

    return zonesdict, outraster
```

Weaving functionality into the user interface

Next, let's make the analysis functionality created so far accessible in the user interface of our application.

Layer-specific right-click functions

In *Chapter 5, Managing and Organizing Geographic Data*, we instructed our application that right-clicking a layer in the LayersPane give us a menu of actions to choose from that is specific to that particular layer. In the current chapter, the only layer-specific functionality we made is the buffer operation. Therefore, we add the buffer menu option to the RightClickMenu_VectorLayer class in app/dialogues.py. Remember to find and save an app/icons/buffer.png icon so that it can be displayed next to the menu's buffer item:

```
        # Buffering
        def open_options_window():
            window = VectorBufferOptionWindow(self.layeritem,
    self.layerspane, self.layeritem, statusbar)
        self.imgs["buffer"] = icons.get("buffer.png", width=32,
    height=32)
        self.add_command(label="Buffer",
    command=open_options_window, image=self.imgs["buffer"],
    compound="left")
```

Defining the tool options windows

Still in app/dialogues.py, we define the layer-specific tool options windows that should pop up. Since they are layer-specific, we add the LayerItem's data as a hidden option that the user shouldn't worry about setting. The only user input here is the buffer distance expression we introduced earlier based on the units of the data's coordinate reference system, which can be either positive for growing or negative for shrinking. An expression calculator may be a nice touch for the user to add here on their own.

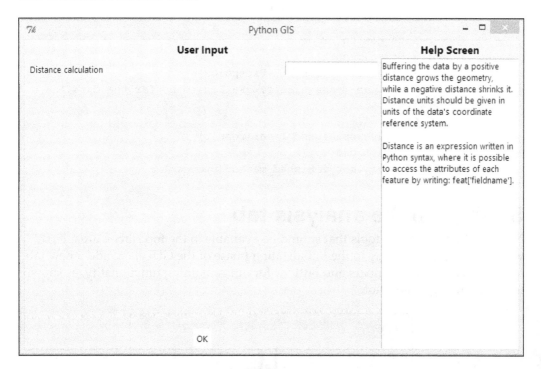

Here is the code for the mentioned functionality:

```
class VectorBufferOptionWindow(Window):
    def __init__(self, master, layerspane, layeritem, statusbar,
**kwargs):
        # Make this class a subclass and add to it
        Window.__init__(self, master, **kwargs)

        # Create runtoolframe
        self.runtool = RunToolFrame(self)
        self.runtool.pack(fill="both", expand=True)
        self.runtool.assign_statusbar(statusbar)
```

```
                # Add a hidden option from its associated layeritem data
                self.runtool.add_hidden_option(argname="data",
        value=layeritem.renderlayer.data)


                # Set the remaining options
                self.runtool.set_target_method("Buffering data...",
        vector.analyzer.buffer)
                self.runtool.add_option_input(argname="dist_expression",
                                label="Distance calculation",
                                valuetype=str)


                # Define how to process
                def process(result):
                    if isinstance(result, Exception):
                        popup_message(self, "Failed to buffer the data:" +
        "\n\n" + str(result) )
                    else:
                        layerspane.add_layer(result)
                        self.destroy()
                self.runtool.set_finished_method(process)
```

Setting up the analysis tab

Next, we focus on those tools that should be available in the top ribbon area. First,
we go to app/builder.py in the initialization phase of the GUI class, add a new tab
for analysis, and add toolbars and buttons for our remaining functionality, as shown
in the following screenshot:

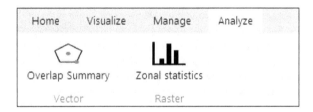

Here is the code to create the **Analyze** tab:

```
        ## Analysis tab
        analysistab = self.ribbon.add_tab("Analyze")
        ### (Vector toolbar)
        vectorfiles = analysistab.add_toolbar("Vector")
        def open_overlapsummary_window():
            window = VectorOverlapSummaryWindow(self,
        self.layerspane, self.statusbar)
```

```
            vectorfiles.add_button(text="Overlap Summary",
icon="overlap.png",
                                command=open_overlapsummary_window)
        ### (Raster toolbar)
        rasterfiles = analysistab.add_toolbar("Raster")
        def open_zonalstats_window():
            window = RasterZonalStatsOptionWindow(self,
self.layerspane, self.statusbar)
        rasterfiles.add_button(text="Zonal statistics",
icon="zonalstats.png",
                                command=open_zonalstats_window)
```

Defining the tool options window

In the tool options window, for overlap summary, we define the standard way in `app/dialogues.py`. Note that the process of adding fieldname statistic tuples for the output should ideally be chosen from two drop-down lists (one for available fieldnames and one for available statistic types). Since we have no such double drop-down widget readily available, we instead settle for having the user spell it out as a tuple with two quote-enclosed strings, which, unfortunately, is not very user friendly. Using double drop-down lists can be an exercise for the reader to implement. Furthermore, since we have no way of visualizing the output data based on their attributes, this method is currently useless within the confines of our application:

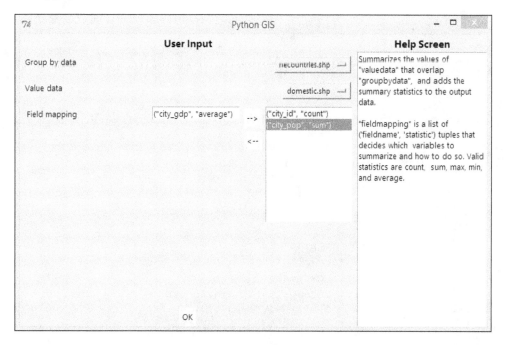

Here is the code to implement the mentioned functionality:

```python
class VectorOverlapSummaryWindow(Window):
    def __init__(self, master, layerspane, statusbar, **kwargs):
        # Make this class a subclass and add to it
        Window.__init__(self, master, **kwargs)

        # Create runtoolframe
        self.runtool = RunToolFrame(self)
        self.runtool.pack(fill="both", expand=True)
        self.runtool.assign_statusbar(statusbar)

        # Set the remaining options
        self.runtool.set_target_method("Calculating overlap
summary on data...", vector.analyzer.overlap_summary)
        def get_data_from_layername(name):
            data = None
            for layeritem in layerspane:
                if layeritem.namelabel["text"] == name:
                    data = layeritem.renderlayer.data
                    break
            return data
        self.runtool.add_option_input(argname="groupbydata",
                            label="Group by data",
                            default="(Choose layer)",
                            choices=[layeritem.namelabel["text"]
for layeritem in layerspane],
                            valuetype=get_data_from_layername)
        self.runtool.add_option_input(argname="valuedata",
                            label="Value data",
                            default="(Choose layer)",
                            choices=[layeritem.namelabel["text"]
for layeritem in layerspane],
                            valuetype=get_data_from_layername)
        self.runtool.add_option_input(argname="fieldmapping",
                            label="Field mapping",
                            multi=True,
                            valuetype=eval)

        # Define how to process
        def process(result):
            if isinstance(result, Exception):
                popup_message(self, "Failed to calculate overlap
summary on data:" + "\n\n" + str(result) )
```

```
        else:
            layerspane.add_layer(result, name="overlap
summary")
        self.runtool.set_finished_method(process)
```

For the zonal statistics tool, we do the same:

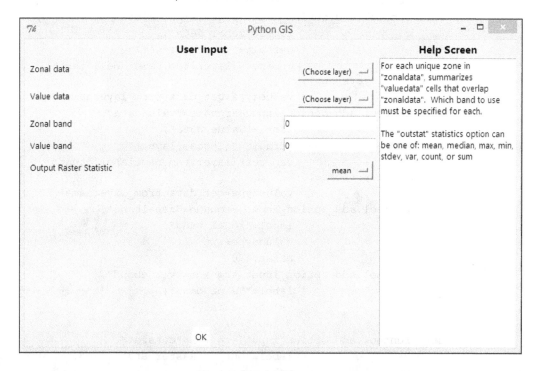

Here is the code to implement the mentioned functionality:

```
class RasterZonalStatsOptionWindow(Window):
    def __init__(self, master, layerspane, statusbar, **kwargs):
        # Make this class a subclass and add to it
        Window.__init__(self, master, **kwargs)

        # Create runtoolframe
        self.runtool = RunToolFrame(self)
        self.runtool.pack(fill="both", expand=True)
        self.runtool.assign_statusbar(statusbar)

        # Set the remaining options
        self.runtool.set_target_method("Calculating zonal
statistics on data...", raster.analyzer.zonal_statistics)
        def get_data_from_layername(name):
```

```
                    data = None
                    for layeritem in layerspane:
                        if layeritem.namelabel["text"] == name:
                            data = layeritem.renderlayer.data
                            break
                    return data
            self.runtool.add_option_input(argname="zonaldata",
                            label="Zonal data",
                            default="(Choose layer)",
                            choices=[layeritem.namelabel["text"]
    for layeritem in layerspane],
                            valuetype=get_data_from_layername)
            self.runtool.add_option_input(argname="valuedata",
                            label="Value data",
                            default="(Choose layer)",
                            choices=[layeritem.namelabel["text"]
    for layeritem in layerspane],
                            valuetype=get_data_from_layername)
            self.runtool.add_option_input(argname="zonalband",
                            label="Zonal band",
                            valuetype=int,
                            default=0)
            self.runtool.add_option_input(argname="valueband",
                            label="Value band",
                            valuetype=int,
                            default=0)
            self.runtool.add_option_input(argname="outstat",
                            label="Output Raster Statistic",
                            valuetype=str,
                            default="mean",

choices=["min","max","count","sum","mean","median","var","stddev"]
        )
```

However, when it is time to process the zonal statistics results, we not only add the output raster as a layer, but also pop up a scrollable window displaying the summary statistics for all the zones. To create the scrollable text widget, Tkinter already has a prebuilt scrollable text widget (which for some odd reason is placed in a module of its own, imported here as tkst), so we use this:

```
        # Define how to process
        def process(result):
            if isinstance(result, Exception):
                popup_message(self, "Failed to calculate zonal
statistics on the data:" + "\n\n" + str(result) )
```

```
        else:
                zonesdict, outraster = result
                # add the resulting zonestatistics layer
                layerspane.add_layer(outraster, name="zonal
statistic")
                # also view stats in window
                win = Window()
                textbox = tkst.ScrolledText(win)
                textbox.pack(fill="both", expand=True)
                textbox.insert(tk.END, "Zonal statistics detailed
result:")
                textbox.insert(tk.END, "\n-----------------------
---------\n")
                for zone,stats in zonesdict.items():
                        statstext = "\n"+"Zone %i:"%zone
                        statstext += "\n\t" + "\n\t".join(["%s:
%f"%(key,val) for key,val in stats.items()])
                        textbox.insert(tk.END, statstext)
        self.runtool.set_finished_method(process)
```

Summary

In this chapter, we added the bare minimum of basic and commonly used GIS analysis tools. Specifically, we added a flexible buffer tool available when right-clicking on a vector layer, and an analysis tab with one button for overlap summary between vector data, and another button for zonal statistics between raster data.

However, this is only barely scratching the surface of the types of analyses one can do in a GIS application, and the fun part comes when you choose to take the application further and build additional functionalities. For instance, how you can link tools together to simplify the steps needed and create custom analysis tools that help you, or your intended target audience, become more efficient.

With the completion of the analysis component of our application, we are left with a very simple but functional GIS application that works, at least for demonstration purposes. In order for the application to be usable outside of our own development environment, especially to non-programmers, you must turn our attention to making it a self-contained application, which is what we will do in the next chapter.

7
Packaging and Distributing Your Application

We have now arrived at the final step in our application development process. We have a working application that contains a number of basic GIS features. However, so far, it can only be run on our own computer in the very specific development environment we have set up. If you want people besides yourself to benefit from your application or just to make it easier for you to travel with and use your application on multiple computers, you need to package the application so it can be more easily installed. In this chapter, we will walk through this final steps of:

- Assigning an icon to be displayed as the logo of our application
- Converting your development environment to a self-contained folder structure with an executable (.exe) file for running your application
- Giving your application an installer wizard for a more permanent installation

Attaching an application logo

Up until now, you have probably noticed that our application is shown with a small rather generic-looking red icon in the top left of the window and down by the list of open applications. This is the standard Tkinter logo used for all Tkinter GUI applications made in Python including the IDLE editor. For your own application, you will obviously want your own icon.

The icon image file

First, you must find or create the icon that you want. Now, in order to assign the logo to your application, you need it to be in a .ico format, a format that contains the same image at multiple different resolutions for optimal display. In all likelihood, the image you created or found will be a normal image file such as .png, .bmp, or .gif, so we need to convert it. We will do this as a one-time process using Python and PIL, since we already have them installed.

Using this PIL approach, there is one small obstacle that we may have to hack our way past. The online documentation for py2exe (the package we will be using to create an EXE file for our application) warns us that in order to assign an icon to the EXE file, it matters in what order the various resolutions of the icon file are saved. The sizes must be assigned in order of largest to smallest, otherwise it won't work.

We come across an obstacle in PIL, in version 2.8.1 or lower, where it automatically orders image sizes in reverse order of smallest to largest behind the scenes, regardless of the order you originally specify. Luckily, the PIL/Pillow development team were very responsive when I raised the issue, so the problem has already been fixed and should no longer be a problem once the next stable version 2.8.2 is released.

If the new patched PIL version is not out yet, it is still easy to fix on our own. Brave as we are, we dive into the internal working files of PIL, located in C:/Python27/ Lib/site-packages/PIL. In the IcoImagePlugin.py file, towards the top of the script, there is a _save function. There you will see that it sorts the specified sizes argument from smallest to largest with the following code: sizes = sorted(sizes, key=lambda x: x[0]). All we have to do is delete or comment out that line so that it is entirely up to the user in which order the sizes are saved.

Now, we are ready to convert your chosen logo image. We only need to do this once and it is fairly easy, so we do this in the interactive Python Shell window instead of the usual file editor. If you are already in the Python IDLE file editor, just click on **Run** from the Python Shell in the top menu. Essentially we just import PIL, load your chosen image file, and save it to a new file with the .ico extension. When saving, we give it the sizes argument containing a list of width-height tuples with the standard icon resolutions we want to support, in the descending order. It makes sense to save this icon image in the pythongis/app folder. Run the following commands:

```
>>> import PIL, PIL.Image
>>> img = PIL.Image.open("your/path/to/icon.png")
>>> img.save("your/path/to/pythongis/app/icon.ico",
sizes=[(255,255),(128,128),(64,64),(48,48),(32,32),(16,16),(8,8)])
```

Assigning the icon

Now that we have the icon file, we can assign it to our application. This is done by assigning the icon to Tkinter which will place our icon in the top-left corner of our application window and down by the Windows taskbar of active applications. We do this in `app/builder.py` in the `run` function, simply by pointing our root application window to the path of our icon. The icon file is in the same folder as `app/builder.py`, so one may think that a relative path to `logo.ico` will suffice, but apparently for this particular task of assigning a GUI icon, Tkinter requires a full absolute path. For this, we take advantage of the global `__file__` variable, which points to the absolute path of the running script:

```
# assign logo from same directory as this file
import sys, os
curfolder,curfile = os.path.split(__file__)
logopath = os.path.join(curfolder, "logo.ico")
window.iconbitmap(logopath)
```

If you run the application now, you should see that the icon appears in the top-left corner and at the bottom. Although we have told Tkinter to use the icon inside the application itself, this will not affect what the EXE file will look like when we browse and view the file in Windows explorer. We will now see how this is done as we move onto packaging and creating the EXE file.

The application start up script

Since we want an EXE file that opens and runs our application, we need a script that explicitly defines how to start up our application. Our `guitester.py` script that we have used for testing purposes throughout the book does exactly that. So we take our testing script and, for the sake of clarity, rename it to `mygisapp.py` (or whatever you wish to call your app). The folder location of our main `pythongis` folder should then look like this:

Since all we did was rename our previous `guitester.py` script to `mygisapp.py`, the content should remain unchanged and it will look like this:

```
import pythongis as pg
pg.app.run()
```

Packaging your application

With the application startup defined, we are now ready for packaging it. Packaging our application means that our application becomes self-contained with all the necessary files grouped into one folder tree (that are currently spread out across numerous locations on your computer), along with an EXE file that the user can double-click on to run the application.

Installing py2exe

There are numerous libraries in Python for packaging projects, and here we choose to use py2exe since it is very easy to install:

1. Go to `www.py2exe.org`.

2. Click on the **Download** link at the top, which takes you to
   `http://sourceforge.net/projects/py2exe/files/py2exe/0.6.9/`.

3. Download and run the latest version for Python 2.7, which is currently
   `py2exe-0.6.9.win32-py2.7.exe`.

> py2exe is specific to the Windows platform; you have to build on Windows and your program can only be used on Windows.
>
> Another alternative for Windows will be PyInstaller:
> `http://pythonhosted.org/PyInstaller/`.
>
> The equivalent for Mac OS X is py2app:
> `https://pythonhosted.org/py2app/`.
>
> For Linux you can use cx_Freeze:
> `http://cx-freeze.sourceforge.net/`.

Developing a packaging strategy

There are many ways to package an application, so before we go diving in we should first understand how py2exe works and plan a packaging strategy accordingly. Given a script that the user wants to package, what py2exe does is run through the script detecting all import statements recursively and thus which libraries must be included in the final package. It then creates a folder called `dist` (it also creates one called `build` but that one is irrelevant for us) which becomes the distributable folder that contains all the required files and an EXE file that runs our application based on our startup script.

A crucial decision is how we choose to bundle our package. We can either bundle most of the required files and dependencies into the EXE file itself or a ZIP file, or not bundle anything by keeping everything loose in a folder structure. At first, bundling may seem like the neatest and best organized choice. Unfortunately, py2exe (as with other packaging libraries) often does not correctly detect or copy all the necessary files from dependencies (especially the .dll and .pyc files), leading to a startup failure of our application. There are options we can specify to help py2exe detect and include everything correctly, but this can get tedious for large projects and still might not let us correct every error. By leaving everything as files and folders instead of bundling it away, we can actually go in and correct some of the mistakes made by py2exe after it has done its work.

We get greater control with the non-bundle approach because the EXE file becomes like the Python interpreter, and everything in the top level of the dist folder becomes like Python's site-packages folder for importable libraries. This way, by manually copying dependencies in full from site-packages to the dist folder they become importable in the same way that they do when Python usually imports them from site-packages. py2exe will detect and handle correctly our imports of built-in Python libraries, but for the more advanced third-party dependencies, including our main pythongis library, we want to add them ourselves. We can put this strategy into practice when we next create the build script.

Creating the build script

To package a project, py2exe needs a very simple script of instructions. Save this as setup.py in the same directory that our main pythongis folder is located in. Here is the hierarchical directory structure:

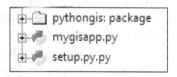

We start our setup.py file by linking to the mygisapp.py startup script that should be run by the EXE file, and point to the path of our icon file so that the EXE file will look like that when browsing. Under options, we set skip_archive to True following our non-bundle strategy. We also prevent py2exe from trying to read and copy two binary files from the pyagg package that lead to errors that aren't actually necessary because they are only provided for cross-version and cross-platform portability.

If you meet other build errors as your application evolves, ignoring such errors using dll_excludes for the .dll and .pyd files or excludes for modules or packages can be a good way to ignore those, and instead copy-paste the required files after building. Following is the code for the procedures we just described, as written in the setup.py script:

```
############
### allow building the exe by simply running this script
import sys
sys.argv.append("py2exe")

############
### imports
from distutils.core import setup
import py2exe

###########
### options
WINDOWS = [{"script": "mygisapp.py",
            "icon_resources": [(1,"pythongis/app/logo.ico")] }]
OPTIONS = {"skip_archive": True,
           "dll_excludes": ["python26.dll","python27.so"],
           "excludes": [] }

############
### build
setup(windows=WINDOWS,
      options={"py2exe": OPTIONS}
      )
```

The setup function will build the dist folder next to setup.py and the pythongis folder. As we stated previously in our packaging strategy, py2exe might not copy all of our third-party libraries correctly if they have an advanced layout of files such as the .dll, .pyd, images, or other data files. Therefore, we choose to add some additional code to the script that copies and overwrites the more advanced dependencies such PIL, Pyagg, Rtree, and Shapely from site-packages (assuming you did not install them to some other location), as well as our entire pythongis library, over to the dist folder after the build process. You must make sure the path to site-packages matches your platform.

```
###########
### manually copy pythongis package to dist
### ...because py2exe may not copy all files
import os
import shutil
frompath = "pythongis"
```

```
topath = os.path.join("dist","pythongis")
shutil.rmtree(topath) # deletes the folder copied by py2exe
shutil.copytree(frompath, topath)

###########
### and same with advanced dependencies
### ...only packages, ie folders
site_packages_folder = "C:/Python27/Lib/site-packages"
advanced_dependencies = ["PIL", "pyagg", "rtree", "shapely"]
for dependname in advanced_dependencies:
    frompath = os.path.join(site_packages_folder, dependname)
    topath = os.path.join("dist", dependname)
    shutil.rmtree(topath) # deletes the folder copied by py2exe
    shutil.copytree(frompath, topath)
```

With the `setup.py` script created, you simply run the script to package your application. It may take a minute or two for py2exe to copy everything. Once finished, there will be a `dist` folder available in the same folder as `setup.py` and `pythongis`:

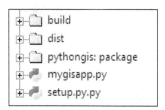

Inside the `dist` folder, there will be a `mygisapp.exe` file (assuming that was the name of your startup script) that should look like your chosen icon, and that when run, should successfully launch your similarly iconified application window. While inside the `dist` folder, check to see that py2exe did not accidentally include any libraries that you were trying to avoid. For instance, Shapely has optional support for and will try to import NumPy when available, which causes py2exe to add it to your `dist` folder even if you do not use it. Avoid this by adding the unwanted packages to the setup script's excludes option.

Adding the visual C runtime DLL

If you are doing this on Windows, there is one last crucial step before our application is fully standalone. The Python programming environment relies on a Microsoft Visual C runtime DLL that was included when we installed Python. However, many versions of this DLL exist, so not all computers or users will have the specific one that our application needs. py2exe will not include the required DLL by default, so it is up to us to include it in our `dist` folder. Including the DLL in your installation is a simple matter of copy and paste, using the following steps:

1. Although we should technically already have the DLL somewhere on our computer, I think there is enough variability and pitfalls with finding the correct one that it is best to get it by doing a clean install of the (free) Microsoft Visual C redistributable program. Download and install the version that your version of Python uses, for which 32-bit Python 2.7 is **Microsoft Visual C++ 2008 Redistributable Package (x86)**, available from `http://www.microsoft.com/download/en/details.aspx?displaylang=en&id=29`.

 For an overview of other Python versions and bit architectures and their required VC++ and DLL versions, see this excellent post:

`http://stackoverflow.com/questions/9047072/windows-python-version-and-vc-redistributable-version`

2. Once installed, go to the folder of your new installation, which should be something like `C:\Program Files\Microsoft Visual Studio 9.0\VC\redist\x86\`, although this may vary depending on your version and bit-architecture.

3. Once there, you will find a folder called `Microsoft.VC90.CRT` containing the following files:
   - `Microsoft.VC90.CRT.manifest`
   - `msvcm90.dll`
   - `msvcp90.dll`
   - `msvcr90.dll`

   As part of the free license, Microsoft requires that you include that entire folder with your application, so go ahead and copy it to your `dist` folder.

4. Now, your EXE file should always be able to find the required DLLs. If you experience trouble or want more information, check out the DLL section of the official py2exe tutorial at `http://www.py2exe.org/index.cgi/Tutorial#Step5`.

You have now successfully packaged your application and made it portable! Notice how the entire application only weighs a mere 30 MB, making it a breeze to upload, download, or even email. If you built your application and the package using 32-bit Python as recommended, your program should work on any Windows 7 or 8 computer (they are essentially the same in the eyes of Python and EXE files). This includes both 32-bit and 64-bit Windows, since 64-bit code is backwards-compatible with 32-bit code. If you used 64-bit Python, it will only work for those who have 64-bit Windows, which is not ideal.

Creating an installer

At this point, you can theoretically slap your `dist` folder on a USB stick as a portable GIS application or share it with others by means of a ZIP archive. This is fine up to a certain point, but is not the most professional or credible way to distribute your application if you are aiming for a wider audience. In order to run the application, the user, including yourself, has to locate the EXE file far down the long list of oddly named files they don't understand. This is just too much of the gory details and manual work that should have come straight out of the box.

More often, people are used to receiving an installer file that guides the user to install the program in a more permanent location and that creates the shortcuts from them. This not only seems more professional, but also takes care of the more advanced steps for the user. As the final step, we will create such an installer for our GIS application, using the widely recommended installation software **Inno Setup**.

Installing Inno Setup

To install Inno Setup, use the following steps:

1. Go to `http://www.jrsoftware.org/`.
2. Click on the **Inno Setup** link on the left side.
3. Click on the **Downloads** link on the left side.
4. Under the stable heading, download and install the file called `isetup-5.5.5.exe`.

Setting up your application's installer

Once you run the Inno Setup, you will be prompted with a welcome screen where you should choose **Create a new script file using the Script Wizard**, as shown in the following screenshot:

This gives you a step-by-step wizard, where you will do the following:

1. On the first screen of the wizard, leave the checkbox unchecked and click on **Next**.

2. On the second screen, provide the name and version of the application, as well as the publisher name and a website if applicable.

3. On the third, screen leave the default install locations.

4. The fourth screen is the most crucial one: you tell the installer the location of your EXE file and the location of your entire self-contained `dist` folder by clicking on **Add folder** (which you should probably rename to the name of your application).

5. On the fifth screen, leave the default start menu options.

6. On the sixth screen, you can provide a license text file, and/or some custom information text to display at the beginning and end of the installation.

7. On the seventh screen, choose the language of the installer.

8. On the eight screen, set **Custom compiler output folder** to your application name (the name of the program folder once installed), **Compiler output base file name** (the name of the installer file) to [your-application-name]_ setup, and **Custom Setup icon file** to the icon we created earlier.

9. On the ninth screen, click on **Finish** to create the installer.

10. When prompted to save the setup script, choose **Yes** and save it alongside your setup.py script, so you can rebuild or modify the installer later.

With this, you should now have a setup file bearing your icon that guides the user through installing your newly made GIS application. All of your hard work is now neatly wrapped into a single file, and can finally be shared and used by a broader audience.

Summary

In this chapter, you completed the final packaging step of creating your GIS application. You gave the application a finishing touch by giving it a logo icon to be displayed on the executable file and as part of the application window. We then packaged the application in a self-contained folder that can be run on any Windows 7 or 8 computer (including both 32- and 64-bit systems, provided you used 32-bit Python). Finally, we gave it a professional touch by making an install wizard for a more "official" introduction and installation of your application. The end users of your application do not need to know Python programming or the fact that it was used to make the program. The only thing they need is to run your friendly setup file, and they can begin using your application by clicking on the newly added shortcuts on their Windows desktop or start menu.

Having completed the steps of making a simple GIS application in Python from start to finish, follow on to the last chapter, as we quickly look back at the lessons learned, and consider possible paths and tips for you to further extend and customize your very own application.

8
Looking Forward

Congratulations! You are now a proud owner of your very own GIS application; but not really. In reality, you have only started the journey. The application we created is still very basic, and while it has some of the core essential features, it lacks many others. You probably also have a few ideas and customizations that you want to implement on your own. Before we send you off to fend for yourself, in this final chapter we will look at some of the ways that you can move forward with your application:

- Areas where the existing user interface should be improved

- Some tips on building alternative GUI layouts using our toolkit

- Suggestions for additional GIS functionality to add to the application

- How to go about supporting your application on additional platforms such as Mac and mobile devices

Improvements to the user interface

In the application, we made in this book, we tried to give it a modern and intuitive design. However, since we had to balance this with also building GIS content, there are several user interface aspects we were not able to address.

Saving and loading user sessions

One obvious thing that is missing from our general user interface is that we have no way to save or load a user session. That is, saving the current state of loaded layers and their properties, the sequence of layers, general map options, projection, zoom level, and so on, so that we can return to the same application session we previously used. The **Home** tab will be a good place for a load and save session button, which can also be called on with the keyboard shortcuts *Ctrl + O* and *Ctrl + S*.

In order to save these settings, we will have to come up with a file format specification as well as an identifiable filename extension. This can be, for instance, a simple JSON text file ending with .pgs (short for Python GIS if that is the name of your application) containing a dictionary or dictionaries of options. Layers can be reloaded based on their origin file path, and perhaps the user can be forced to save to file any virtual layers.

File drag and drop

Adding data layers with the **Add Layer** button is fine, but sometimes it can be a hassle to have to repeatedly locate the files each time, especially if they are located in deeply nested folders in multiple locations. Dragging and dropping series of files from already opened Windows folders to the application window is often a preferred way to add layers. Currently, we have not added any support for this in our application because Tkinter has no built-in support for detecting drag and drop between applications.

 Luckily, there exists a Tk extension for this called TkDND at SourceForge which you will have to setup: http://sourceforge.net/projects/ tkdnd/. The following Python wrapper posted on StackOverflow should let you access this Tk extension in your Tkinter application: http:// stackoverflow.com/questions/14267900/python-drag-and- drop-explorer-files-to-tkinter-entry-widget.

GUI widgets

A great deal of our application framework has been spent tweaking and creating our own custom widget templates, for the purposes of widget styling and code reusability. As you move forward, I suggest following this logic even further so it becomes easier for you to build and extend the user interface. For instance, in our RunToolFrame, we created a method that will add commonly needed combinations of widgets inside that particular frame. However, to make it even more flexible you can make these into widget classes of their own so you can place them anywhere inside your application. In particular, I would suggest adding scrollbars to your widgets, which is something our current application is lacking.

On a more superficial note, although Tkinter generally has a nice look, especially with custom styling, some of our application widgets still look a bit out of place, such as the drop-down choice menu. With some style experimentation though, you should be able to improve its look. Alternatively, Python 2.7 and newer versions come packaged with a Tkinter extension module called **ttk**, which provides a newer looking ComboBox drop-down widget, among many others. The only difference that you should note, if you choose to switch to ttk widgets is that, they are styled using a different approach that requires you to make changes to the old Tkinter based code.

Other variations of the user interface

The beauty of our approach to building a flexible toolkit of GIS-related widgets, is that they can be used, positioned, and combined in any number of ways, rather than locking ourselves to the traditional "LayersPane-MapView" layout of a GIS. For instance, here are some interesting examples of useful ways to create different types of GIS applications and layouts.

Instead of just a single-map GIS application, you can split the window into multiple windows, say 2 or 4 maps with a LayersPane in the middle. By connecting each map to the same LayerGroup and LayersPane, the layer sequence and symbolizations you define there will affect all of the maps, but with the added benefit that you can have multiple eyes on the same data, at different locations and zoom levels. Refer to the following screenshot:

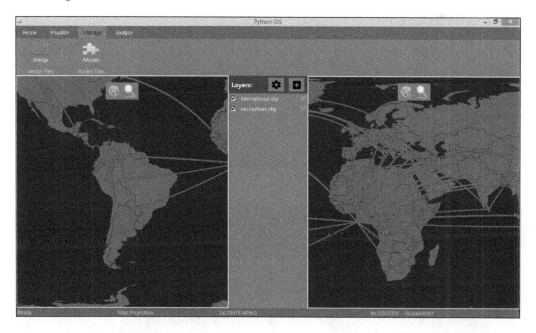

Alternatively, you don't have to have all of the widgets there at all. You can create a minimalistic map-only application, where layers can be preloaded and/or managed in a different or a more discrete way. Alternatively, you can have a more management-oriented application with only the LayersPane and the functionality to manage and organize your files.

Finally, remember that all of our widgets are styled and easily changed based on color and font instructions in our app/toolkit/theme.py module. We built it like that for a reason, so make use of it!

Adding more GIS functionality

There are loads of GIS functionalities that you may wish to add to your application. Of the many pre-existing modules and libraries available, here are just a few suggestions as to what is mostly needed and possible to do. A more comprehensive list can be found at www.pythongisresources.wordpress.com or on the Python Package Index website.

 For more in-depth implementations of some of these tools, and further reading and ideas on how to implement a GIS application in Python, refer to *Python Geospatial Development - Second Edition* by Erik Westra.

Basic GIS selections

There are a few core data selection functions that we have still not implemented. Importantly, these include the ability to subset a layer based on a data query, or spatially cropping it based on a region bounding box or overlap with another layer. Both of these should be as simple as looping through the features and only keeping the matches from the attribute query or spatial query. The ability to view the actual information stored in vector data is also something we are currently lacking, such as in a table or with a feature identification tool where the user can click on any vector feature or raster cell and view their attributes or values.

More advanced visualization

Currently, our application is not very flexible when it comes to visualizing data. Vector data is rendered with a single random color for all features, and rasters as greyscale or RGB, with no ability to change it. However, using our RunToolFrame widget, it should be easy to pack it inside a **Symbology** ribbon tab in the layer's properties window and assign input widgets and a function that updates that layer's styleoptions dictionary and redraws it.

Even with this though, a hallmark of GIS visualization is that we should also be able to have these colors and sizes vary based on each vector feature's attributes in order to visualize patterns. Similarly, we need to be able to label layers by rendering text over each feature based on its attributes. Finally, we should be able to add cartographic elements to the map such as adding a custom title, placing a legend, a scale, and a north arrow. These are some very exciting areas that you can work on improving.

Online data services

For our application, we built the capability to load data by pointing it to a file path on your computer, which is the traditional way of working in a GIS. But it is increasingly common to load generic background data or regularly updated data feeds such as satellite imagery directly from the web, via the **Open Geospatial Consortium** (**OGC**) web service interface standard.

In Python, I would recommend using OWSLib which lets you access a wide variety of online services and data sources, and has great documentation for learning more about it.

> For a more concrete example, see how PyEarthquake uses web services for retrieving real-time earthquake data:
>
> `http://blog.christianperone.com/?p=1013`

Converting between raster and vector data

The ability to convert from a raster grid to vector data of square polygons or center points for more custom processing, or to convert from vector data to a raster grid of a given resolution, is frequently needed. Both of these are currently missing from our application, but should be fairly easy and useful to implement within our existing framework. Rasterizing vector data is essentially the same as drawing it on an image, so you can just draw it to the desired raster resolution using PIL or PyAgg. To vectorize raster data, you can loop through the cells of your raster and create a point geometry at each cell's x and y coordinates (or polygon geometry based on the cell bounding box). Alternatively, you can use GDAL that already has functions for both rasterizing and vectorizing.

Projections

As it currently stands, our application can process and visualize data defined in any projection, but it cannot convert between these projections. So if multiple data have different projections, then there is no way to position or analyze them correctly in relation to each other. Luckily, PyProj is an excellent and widely used Python package based on PROJ4 for converting coordinates from one projection to another and is fairly lightweight. With this, you can add tools to define and convert layer projections and to set on-the-fly reprojection of all layers into a common map projection.

The most difficult part is that there are numerous formats in which projections are stored, such as EPSG codes, OGC URN codes, ESRI WKT, OGC WKT, +proj strings, and GeoTIFF definitions, to name but a few. PyProj requires that projections be defined as +proj strings, so the challenge will be to correctly detect, parse, and convert whichever projection format a file is stored in, over to +proj format. GDAL is the best way to handle these translations, or using `http://www.spatialreference.org` if you only expect to receive codes such as EPSG.

Geocoding

Today, geocoding of addresses and other textual information into coordinates is relatively easy using free online search websites and their programming-friendly APIs. GeoPy is a Python package that provides access to numerous online geocoding services, such as OpenStreetMap, Google, Bing, and many others. This can be added to your application either as a tool for geocoding a table based on a field containing textual locations, or by providing an interactive geocoding search widget that shows the resulting matches on the map.

Going the GDAL/NumPy/SciPy route

If you, at some point, decide to add GDAL, NumPy, and SciPy as dependencies to your application, it will add about 100 MB of additional size to your application, but will also open up a lot of new doors. For instance, the problem of translating between different projection formats will be solved by functions available in GDAL. Adding GDAL and NumPy will also let you add a host of new data loading and saving capabilities, and especially open up for raster management, analysis, and resampling methods using packages like PyResample, RasterStats, and even raster interpolation via SMEAR. For vector data, it will also open the door for more advanced spatial statistic and hotspot analysis as available in PySAL or various clustering algorithms using PyCluster. Matplotlib combined with Basemap or Cartopy may provide all the visual projection support you need without much extra work on your end.

Expanding to other platforms

For now, I can attest that the application works on Windows 7 and even Windows 8 (single-touch navigation of the MapView is especially fun). However, at some point you may find yourself needing to share your GIS application on platforms other than Windows. Python and most of our application's dependencies are in principle cross-platform, and I have personally tested that the application framework that I created over the course of this book also worked on a Mac OS X, though with slightly different installation instructions.

When you are finished creating your application and are ready to distribute it, just get a hold of the operating system that you want to support, install the necessary third-party libraries, and copy and paste your application folder. If the application works from within Python, then just wrap it all up with one of the packaging libraries for your operating system that were suggested in *Chapter 7, Packaging and Distributing Your Application*.

Touch devices

A more trendy and exciting possibility is to be able to port your application to the newer wave of recreational tablets and other mobile touch devices. Our current Tkinter user interface approach is unfortunately not able to be packaged for use on, or contain multitouch gesture support for, phones like Android or iPhone or tablets like iPad. If these are your main audiences, you can possibly keep the GIS processing engine, but may wish to switch the user interface to one based on Kivy, a newer GUI package which is gaining in popularity, which supports multitouch inputs, and is said to support packaging for Android, iPhone, and iPad. If you only want to support iOS, then the Pythonista app provides a GUI builder, several core Python packages like PIL, NumPy, and Matplotlib, access to the iOS rendering engine, and even a way to package your application into an app (though you will still have to apply to get it onto the Apple store).

Summary

We started out in this book seeking to create a basic and lightweight GIS application from scratch. As we reach the end of the book, this is exactly what we have done. Based on an underlying codebase of interlinked Python libraries, we have a distributable visual user interface application that can perform basic loading and saving, visualizing, managing, and analysis of spatial data.

At the very least, you picked up a few ideas of how to go about creating one. The best part about it is that you are fully in control of tweaking, modifying, and further developing it. If you have a particular need or a great idea for a custom workflow application, just look to the many tools available and build it yourself. I am very excited to keep using this application framework myself and especially curious to see what kind of GIS applications you will come up with.

Index

Thank you for buying
Python Geospatial
Development Essentials

About Packt Publishing

Packt, pronounced 'packed', published its first book, *Mastering phpMyAdmin for Effective MySQL Management*, in April 2004, and subsequently continued to specialize in publishing highly focused books on specific technologies and solutions.

Our books and publications share the experiences of your fellow IT professionals in adapting and customizing today's systems, applications, and frameworks. Our solution-based books give you the knowledge and power to customize the software and technologies you're using to get the job done. Packt books are more specific and less general than the IT books you have seen in the past. Our unique business model allows us to bring you more focused information, giving you more of what you need to know, and less of what you don't.

Packt is a modern yet unique publishing company that focuses on producing quality, cutting-edge books for communities of developers, administrators, and newbies alike. For more information, please visit our website at www.packtpub.com.

About Packt Open Source

In 2010, Packt launched two new brands, Packt Open Source and Packt Enterprise, in order to continue its focus on specialization. This book is part of the Packt Open Source brand, home to books published on software built around open source licenses, and offering information to anybody from advanced developers to budding web designers. The Open Source brand also runs Packt's Open Source Royalty Scheme, by which Packt gives a royalty to each open source project about whose software a book is sold.

Writing for Packt

We welcome all inquiries from people who are interested in authoring. Book proposals should be sent to author@packtpub.com. If your book idea is still at an early stage and you would like to discuss it first before writing a formal book proposal, then please contact us; one of our commissioning editors will get in touch with you.

We're not just looking for published authors; if you have strong technical skills but no writing experience, our experienced editors can help you develop a writing career, or simply get some additional reward for your expertise.

Python Geospatial Development - Second Edition

ISBN: 978-1-78216-152-3   Paperback: 508 pages

Learn to build sophisticated mapping applications from scratch using Python tools for geospatial development

1. Build your own complete and sophisticated mapping applications in Python.

2. Walks you through the process of building your own online system for viewing and editing geospatial data.

3. Practical, hands-on tutorial that teaches you all about geospatial development in Python.

Learning Geospatial Analysis with Python

ISBN: 978-1-78328-113-8   Paperback: 364 pages

Master GIS and Remote Sensing analysis using Python with these easy to follow tutorials

1. Construct applications for GIS development by exploiting Python.

2. Focuses on built-in Python modules and libraries compatible with the Python Packaging Index distribution system – no compiling of C libraries necessary.

3. This is a practical, hands-on tutorial that teaches you all about Geospatial analysis in Python.

Please check **www.PacktPub.com** for information on our titles

Python Data Visualization Cookbook

ISBN: 978-1-78216-336-7   Paperback: 280 pages

Over 60 recipes that will enable you to learn how to create attractive visualization using Python's most opular libraries

1. Learn how to set up an optimal Python environment for data visualization.

2. Understand the topics such as importing data for visualization and formatting data for visualization.

3. Understand the underlying data and how to use the right visualizations.

Learning Python Data Visualization

ISBN: 978-1-78355-333-4   Paperback: 212 pages

Master how to build dynamic HTML5-ready SVG charts using Python and the pygal library

1. A practical guide that helps you break into the world of data visualization with Python.

2. Understand the fundamentals of building charts in Python.

3. Packed with easy-to-understand tutorials for developers who are new to Python or charting in Python.